THE WAY WE WILL BE

50 years from today

60 of the World's Greatest Minds
Share Their Visions of the Next Half Century

MIKE WALLACE

THOMAS NELSON
Since 1798

NASHVILLE   DALLAS   MEXICO CITY   RIO DE JANEIRO   BEIJING

Published in Nashville, Tennessee, by Thomas Nelson. Thomas Nelson is a registered trademark of Thomas Nelson, Inc.

The views presented in this book are not necessarily the same as those of Thomas Nelson Publishers.

Thomas Nelson, Inc. titles may be purchased in bulk for educational, business, fundraising, or sales promotional use. For information, please email SpecialMarkets@ThomasNelson.com.

Page design: Walter Petrie

Library of Congress Cataloging-in-Publication Data

The way we will be 50 years from today : 60 of the world's greatest minds share their visions of the next half-century / [edited by] Mike Wallace.
    p. cm.
  ISBN 978-0-8499-0370-0
  1. Social prediction. 2. Social indicators. 3. Economic indicators. 4. Political indicators. 5. Health status indicators. 6. Technological forecasting. 7. Quality of life—Forecasting. 8. Twenty-first century—Forecasts. I. Wallace, Mike, 1918–
HM901.W39 2008
303.4909'05—dc22   2007045281

Printed in the United States of America

08 09 10 11 12 QW 5 4 3 2 1

Contents

Introduction

This book presents the future as predicted by people who have brought us the present.

When you ask some of the smartest, most imaginative people on the planet what the world will be like in fifty years, the answers you get are as unexpected as they are visionary.

Predicting the future isn't easy. As one physicist who contributed to this collection pointed out, when you normally deal with what the universe will be like in tens of billions of years, guessing what the world will be like in fifty years requires a completely different way of thinking.

The Internet is only decades old; commercial television broadcasting has only been around since 1941; human viruses were discovered just seventy-five years ago. Smallpox was eliminated in 1977, and the cell phone camera was invented in 1997. If you traveled back in time to fifty years before these things were invented, you'd find the world of the future hard to envision.

Fifty years from now is just around the corner—it's a little over twenty-six million minutes from now, but those minutes tick by quickly. This is the world our children and grandchildren will be living in. It's a world of amazing medical and technological miracles that's truly mind-boggling. Diseases that kill millions will be vanquished. We will explore mysterious places in the solar system and deep in the oceans. Meteorologists will predict weather not only with uncanny accuracy but almost on a neighborhood-by-neighborhood basis. Super-fast maglev trains will replace many of the means of transportation we use today. Education will be universal and illiteracy a historical artifact. Teleconferencing will be holographic and make you feel like you're actually in the room with people on the other side of the globe. We will live longer and be stronger in our old age. Beauty and function will become closer companions when we build new buildings in our cities. The sun's light will become a major source of electricity on earth. And the United States will finally adopt the metric system.

But it won't be a perfect world. We may not be able to conquer some diseases that plague us now, and new ones may emerge. War will not be eliminated. Nuclear proliferation may make the world even more dangerous. Global inequalities of wealth will persist. Animal species may continue to become extinct. And then there's the environment, and global warming in particular. While dangers lurk in the future, these are problems that, as the visionaries in this book point out, we can reduce or perhaps turn around. The future will be shaped by what we do in the present. We just have to decide what kind of future we want—and create it.

MIKE WALLACE
New York City
Fifty years before 2058

1

Vint Cerf

Vint Cerf is vice president of Google. Known as a "Father of the Internet," his honors include the Presidential Medal of Freedom and the US National Medal of Technology.

AS WE MAY LIVE

It is springtime in Earth's northern hemisphere in 2058. The population of the planet now exceeds eleven billion, not counting scientific outposts on Titan and even a nascent colony on Mars. Global warming has taken its toll on the coastal areas, and the population has had to move inland in many places. Major landmarks are underwater—or nearly so—and the maps of the continental shorelines have changed, in some cases fairly dramatically. Fresh water is scarce in many parts of the world, and desalinization has become a major industry. Where once oil pipelines were laid and gigantic oil tankers plowed furrows in the ocean, now great water tankers and water pipelines take their place. Our energy comes from the sun, the wind, and the atom. The electrical grid is global, and energy is moved from places with an excess to places with a deficit using a global management system that balances the needs of the planet. Incandescent lights are museum pieces and have been replaced by solid state devices that are programmable and provide an infinite variety of colors and patterns—some of them dynamically adapting to music or other sources of changing input. Every building, vehicle, appliance, and person is on the Net, and sensor systems provide holographic, X-ray-like views of everything. Information sharing and mining provide deep awareness of the dynamic state of the world that is modeled and controlled through globally distributed computational networks.

Telepresence is holographic, and sophisticated tracking mechanisms and presentation mechanisms allow groups to "meet" in richly appointed virtual spaces. The crude avatars of the past have been replaced with holographic views of real people interacting in real time. The merger of the real and the virtual is complete. Children learn by exploring virtual spaces that are co-terminal with the real world so that when they perform virtual experiments, they often receive data from real instruments.

Nanotechnology has brought a cornucopia of products and devices from artificial muscles to ocular and spinal implants. Fabrics adapt in myriad ways to local conditions. Commonplace items like utensils and dishes disassemble after use and are reassembled after filtering foreign material. Dishwashers are museum pieces. Buildings are as aware of environmental conditions as they are of occupancy, and adapt accordingly. While teleportation is not possible, information to construct an object can be sent to a nanoconstructor, which reproduces the object faithfully.

High-energy physics and cosmology have merged, and we have long since discovered the Higgs field and detected the particle that produces it. We have learned how mass and inertia are produced, and the fictional inertia-less drive invented by science fiction author Edward E. Smith now seems possible. Meanwhile, the Interplanetary Internet, initially put into operation linking Earth and Mars almost fifty years ago, has expanded as an increasing number of long-lived robotic and manned space missions have multiplied. A score of missions to nearby stars have been launched, and the one to Proxima Centauri is scheduled to arrive there in about ten years' time. A constellation of interferometric laser optical receivers in orbit around the sun has been built to detect signals from the robotic mission once it has arrived and has entered into orbit around the distant star.

We take it for granted that we can converse with each other using any language, and real-time translation takes place automatically. Even groups can interact in this fashion as long as one person talks at a time. Moreover, it is quite common to speak to appliances around the house and office and have our words converted into appropriate commands and queries through computers on the ubiquitous Internet. Of course, talking to yourself is still considered a sign of instability.

Nearly every job today involves information processing in some form because all the manual labor is done by intelligent or semi-intelligent machines. Some of the mid-21st century jobs would be impossible for an early 21st century citizen to understand. Rather like trying to explain "webmaster" to the man in the 1950s gray flannel suit! The rate of scientific advancement and discovery continues to accelerate as increasing amounts of information become accessible on the Net and can be accessed by increasingly sophisticated analytic software. We continue to speculate about the possibility that computers will become as intelligent as humans—possibly becoming the successors to the human race.

2

Francis S. Collins

*Francis S. Collins, MD, PhD, is a geneticist who led the Human
Genome Project, the audacious effort that read out all three billion letters
of the human DNA instruction book. He continues to lead the National
Human Genome Research Institute and is also a leader in emphasizing
the importance of addressing the ethical, legal, and social implications of
genome research. In his recent book,* The Language of God, *he argues
that science and faith are not opposing worldviews but actually are highly
complementary.*

A Revolution in Medicine

For all of human history, we have essentially been ignorant of the details of our
own instruction book, the hereditary material that passes from parent to child.
All that changed in April 2003, when the Human Genome Project completed
its work and revealed the complete DNA sequence of our own species.

All of us are 99.9 percent the same at the DNA level, but that 0.1 percent of
differences also can carry with it the risk of illnesses such as cancer, heart disease, or diabetes. Those specific genetic risk factors are now being revealed,
opening a new window into understanding the causes of illness and providing ideas about prevention.

With the field of genome research moving so quickly, it is difficult to project where we might be in just five or ten years, and trying to look fifty years into the future is truly daunting. Nonetheless, I'll give it a try.

I am quite confident that in fifty years each of us will have a copy of our own complete DNA sequence, incorporated into a highly accurate electronic medical record and accessible from anywhere in the world. Perhaps this will even be encoded on a chip that's been inserted under the skin of the forearm, along with a large amount of other medically important information. That DNA sequence information, unique to each individual, will be the bedrock of a highly effective form of preventive medicine, where most of our medical resources will be focused on keeping people healthy. Monitors in our homes and workplaces will pick up any evidence of a new environmental exposure that might be harmful. An occasional sampling of a drop of blood (or perhaps just saliva) will detect the presence of a long list of biomarkers that might suggest the very beginnings of trouble, offering the opportunity to intervene quickly. Visits to the doctor may seem a bit like *Star Trek,* with sophisticated imaging capabilities that allow precise assessments of any problem in any organ system. If disease occurs despite all of these preventive measures, the treatments available will be much more individualized and precisely targeted, based on a detailed understanding of the molecular basis of illness. Nanotechnology delivery methods will allow the desired treatment to go directly to where it's needed, without causing side effects in other parts of the body.

We will have learned how to reprogram our own cells to compensate for a problem somewhere in the body. If your liver is failing, cells taken from your skin will be induced to take up the slack. If your heart is weakening, new heart muscle cells will be programmed too. Barring deaths from trauma, the average normal human life span will reach triple digits. But immortality will not be in reach: the death rate will still be one per person.

All of these technical advances will run the risk of depersonalizing medicine, but the best physicians, nurses, and other health professionals will still be those who take the time to get to know the people they are caring for, and to provide a human touch. Certainly by fifty years from now, the realization that access to health care ought to be a basic right of all humans will be agreed upon. I only hope there will be significant political will across the world to act upon that principle.

Will all of this high technology result in a change of our views about humanity? Will we see ourselves as molecular machines rather than creatures capable of noble actions and concerns for our fellow human beings? I am not too worried about that. Yes, science will provide us with many opportunities. But people will still be searching for answers to the meaning of life, and most of us will continue to find comfort and joy by discovering God's love and grace.

3

George F. Smoot

George F. Smoot, an astrophysicist, shares the 2006 Nobel Prize in Physics with John Mather. He is on the faculty of the physics department at the University of California at Berkeley and conducts research in astrophysics and observational cosmology at the Lawrence Berkeley National Laboratory. He is co-author (with Keay Davidson) of Wrinkles in Time.

A Tiny Dot in Cosmic Time; A Big Period in Human Time

I work primarily on studying the creation and long-term history of the universe. Fifty years is just a dot on the cosmic scale; however, on a human scale, fifty years can initiate significant change. Innovations, successfully introduced, are increasing at a rapid rate. They are cumulative and build upon each other as well as through the entrepreneurial attitudes of the modern world. This makes predicting the way we will be in fifty years difficult; nonetheless, it is instructive and humbling to try.

We can safely estimate that we will weather a change in our primary transportation fuel. Oil will no longer be as dominant and prevalent as it is today. This will clearly result in several shifts of power as well as attitudes. This is not to say that there have not been shifts in energy sources—e.g., wood to coal, then petroleum and natural gas. However, it has never been on such a scale both in terms of its daily impact on society with increasing energy needs, and its global nature.

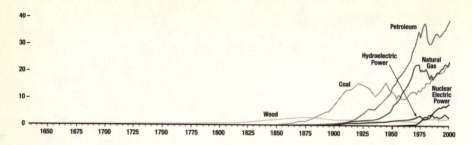

Figure 1. US Energy Consumption by Source, 1635–2000
(QUADRILLION BTU)

We can anticipate that this changeover will be stressful and will bring out both good and bad in our institutions and society. Forward-looking groups have now just begun to grapple with what that might mean for them and their place in society. This is mostly an economic view because predicting the full picture of how this will impact civilization and what directions it will take is very difficult. The ultimate path depends upon many factors, including technology, societal attitudes, accidents of sources, and opportunities. Economic views provide a rationale for making decisions.

One interesting example is the company called BP, formerly known as British Petroleum. Since 2004, it has been advertising itself as BP, standing for "Beyond Petroleum." This is a bold and complicated transition with several nuances. BP anticipates investing some $8 billion in BP Alternative Energy over the next decade, reinforcing its determination to grow its businesses "Beyond Petroleum."

Economic stakes and large sums of money are involved here. Such circumstances require careful thought and planning, as well as the marshalling of resources, for the purpose of inventing and developing innovative technologies that will address complex global energy needs. This is bringing together a generation of scientists deeply knowledgeable in all areas related to bioenergy. This includes the sciences and technology that one would normally expect and especially those that are important for the genetic modifications and viability to develop plants that are efficient and effective bioenergy sources. For this overall investment to be successful, the team must develop the capability to produce, select, and insert the genes into plants and then raise them in quantity and quality, turn them into crops, and then into biofuels. This is not an isolated science team working in the lab, but a large, coordinated effort to go beyond that and put it into large-scale practice within fifty years. This would readily meet my definition for a successful innovation.

Why will this change the way we are? Will having something like ethanol in my car's tank change my life that much? Well, yes, indirectly by the shifts in power and the longer implications for global warming. However, this same basic technology can revolutionize many things: food crops, landscape plants, even biological houses. There are already signs that this approach will first impact health and medicine. The technology to be applied here is first being used to develop a low-cost cure for malaria via genetically modified bacteria that are used to make the cure. Much more will follow in this area. I anticipate a very significant increase in human life span as a result and hope that I will be one of the many beneficiaries. It is quite possible that nearly everyone reading this essay will in fifty years be young (that is, less than 150 years old and in relatively good health). This rapid increase in healthy life span will have a major impact on society. There are already huge shocks from a relative few years' increase in life expectancy.

These are myriad changes, but underneath will we still be the same old humans simply seeking to improve and optimize our lives given the better resources available?

I think that at the same time, we will begin to see a change in the basic human being.

Given that society can routinely re-engineer plants and animals to improve them or utilize them more effectively, what about humans? Clearly, there will be some activity in this area. First, it will come through gene therapy of human genetic diseases. Parents already have some ability to choose whether to have children that have severe genetic defects. It is already partially possible to select not only the sex of one's child (e.g., see the effect of China's one child policy) but also to screen out genetic defects. Even more direct intervention and selection will soon be possible. At the beginning, people with family histories of severe genetic diseases will seek this out. Will not some parents choose a stronger selection for good looks and greater intelligence or other traits likely to make their child more successful in general competition? I think that this is likely as there is evidence that people choose their mates (genetic source for their child) based upon these traits. Every time I have talked to groups of high school or college students, at least a few percent say that if gene enhancement for their forthcoming children were reasonably affordable and safe, they would choose that advantage. It seems to me that on the scale of fifty years, we could see something on the order of 5 to 10 percent of the children being born genetically enhanced, most likely by selection, but also possibly by direct genetic engineering. Once we reach that level, then such advantages go beyond fashion and status into direct competition in the gene pool, much like mate selection. Concerned parents quite often spend large resources (money and time) to ensure that their children have a good education—private schools are a prime example. One could consider simply doubling the human genome (so it would be roughly half the size of the wheat genome), and including all the knowledge up through a great college education directly in the child. No worry about the quality of the teachers, school, or whether the child is studying and paying attention. All that knowledge is there and in place in every cell at one-tenth the cost and many times the reliability.

We may also see societies or groups that believe that the development of enhanced humans—thinkers, wise leaders, great movie stars, etc.—is the wave of the future toward a more utopian society or toward one with distinct economic and strategic advantages. Any of these motivations leads toward genetically modified humans. In fifty years we will likely be at the start of a new, rapid evolution of mankind. One of the motivations will be comparison and competition with the rapidly advancing intelligence of machines. Humans will have to advance significantly to keep pace and even be partners in relationship to machines (machines that were once man's servants). Presumably one feature that these newer humans will have is a better interface to powerful computing. This is a change that will really accelerate innovations that change society and humans. It is interesting to speculate what will mark the turning point when evolution brings us from humans toward the next level.

4

Christian de Duve

Christian de Duve, founder of the International Institute of Cellular and Molecular Pathology in Belgium, shared the Nobel Prize in Medicine in 1974 for describing the structure and function of organelles in biological cells.

WHAT'S AHEAD: "FIGURES DON'T LIE"

If our children and grandchildren keep letting nature follow its course, the situation fifty years from today can only be dramatically worse than it is now. Driven by their ingrained compulsion to reproduce and fight for their own, humans will have gone on multiplying, possibly exceeding the eight-billion mark.

To ensure their survival, they will have reclaimed a good part of the remaining virgin land for growing crops and raising livestock, favoring further desertification and reducing biodiversity. They will have depleted the oceans, lakes, and rivers of much of marine life, to the point of seriously endangering the survival of many species. In their efforts to let everyone share the bounties of technical progress, they will have extended to much of the developing world the equipment and facilities enjoyed by developed countries, from power plants and factories to railroads, airports, highways, and bridges; from trains, ships, and aircraft to motor cars and trucks; from hospitals to water purification and sewage treatment stations; from bathrooms and refrigerators to television sets, telephones, and computers, not to mention toasters, microwave ovens, and dishwashers—all highly commendable but at an enormous environmental cost.

To satisfy their growing need for energy, humans will have exhausted most of the coal and oil reserves of the planet and added many pollutants to the environment. Most likely, they will have been unable to oppose the greenhouse effect in time to prevent major climate changes and the loss of many coastal areas to the rising waters from melting polar ices.

All these hardships, further exacerbated by economic disparities, nationalisms, and religious fundamentalisms, will have heightened the tensions among different groups and populations. Oppositions between haves and have-nots, powerful and weak, believers and unbelievers will have worsened. Large cities, crushed by overcrowding, will have degenerated into jungles ruled by crime and violence. Major conflicts will have continued to rage in various parts of the world. Perhaps even a nuclear powder keg will already have exploded somewhere, killing millions and turning entire countries into ashes.

Large cities, crushed by overcrowding, will have degenerated into jungles ruled by crime and violence.

There is nothing unexpected in this dismal view; it is none other than the extrapolation of the present into the future. It is not an apocalyptic picture conjured by some prophet of doom, but the expression of a stark reality. The handwriting is already on the wall. Humans *are* multiplying almost unrestrainedly, while their habitat is shrinking. Natural resources *are* being depleted; some, like fossil fuels, already nearing exhaustion. Biodiversity *is* being threatened. Species *are* becoming extinct in ever-increasing numbers. The environment *is* being polluted. Climate *is* changing. Cities *are* straining under the pressure of their growing populations to the point of becoming ungovernable, if not unlivable. Want and despair *are* driving increasing numbers to immigrate into affluent countries by any means and at any cost, against rising resistance. Conflict and strife *are* everywhere, supported by an increasingly powerful and uncontrolled technology of death. The specter of a nuclear holocaust no longer belongs to the unthinkable. If unchecked, this movement is bound to snowball in self-accelerating fashion, eventually becoming irreversible. Perhaps not as short a time as fifty years, but not much more could suffice to bring the human-ruled and human-plundered world to the point of no return.

Can something be done to avoid this catastrophic fate? There are some who see the solution in technical progress. Let nuclear fusion be domesticated, and energy becomes inexhaustible. Let hydrogen be developed as fuel, and combustion becomes entirely nonpolluting. And so on. Such developments are no doubt desirable and may well, if achieved in time, provide a welcome relief to some of the looming crises. But numbers cannot be evaded. The living space offered by our planet is limited and must inevitably fail to accommodate an expanding humankind at some stage, whatever the available technologies. Colonization of the Moon or of other celestial bodies has been suggested as a possible way to extend our habitat. It is, however, doubtful that the technologies needed for this could be developed in time to avoid the predicted disasters. Furthermore, there are stringent physical limits to the space that could be gained in this way, if it is to support human life.

There are some who advocate the opposite solution. Let us abandon our technological civilization, they recommend, and go back to nature. Few of those, however, are ready to give up all the benefits of modernity, such as healthy food, vaccines for their children, life-saving drugs, and so on, or even could do without those benefits if they attempted to renounce them. The hardiness of our hunter-gatherer ancestors has long been lost. Today's "back to nature" communes can live only in enclaves surrounded and supported by a technological society.

Not the least objection to the "back to nature" solution is that it rests on a faulty premise. Nature is not good or benevolent. Neither is it bad. It is neutral and, especially, totally improvident. Nature does no more than blindly favor those forms of life that are best able to survive and produce progeny under the prevailing conditions, and it does so in a purely passive fashion, by the sole virtue of immediate benefits and with no regard for long-term consequences.

Natural selection has no foresight. Humans, thanks to their superior brains, have been privileged winners in this game, managing to emerge under almost any conditions. This explains the unique success of the human species, which has invaded the entire planet with ever-increasing throngs, appropriating more and more of the planet's resources for their own use.

For most of human history, this expansion has been allowed to take place without hindrance and even encouraged, driven by the conviction that the earth was ours to enjoy and exploit, and supported by what seemed to be inexhaustible means. It is only in the last century that humankind has begun to suffer from the constraints imposed by natural limits to its unchecked growth. Only in the last few decades has humankind become conscious of this fact and of its menaces for the future. The corresponding feeling of planetary responsibility is barely awakening; it is still far from being a globally shared concern.

This text started with the condition, "If our children and grandchildren keep letting nature follow its course." Humanity's only hope is for our children and grandchildren *not* to let nature follow its course and put *reason* in the lead. This, unlike the rest of the living world, humans have the unique ability to do, though, perhaps, not the necessary wisdom, which, until now, was not a condition of evolutionary success.

Among the many measures that must be taken—and, fortunately, are beginning to be taken or, at least, are contemplated—curbing population expansion, which is the root of all other problems, is the most urgent. If this is not done imperatively and by every available means, natural selection will take care of the matter for us, through famine, disease, genocide, and war. The cost will be exorbitant and may come to exceed what humanity can bear. Those who still oppose birth control, whatever their motivation, should reflect on the dramatic long-term consequences of their militancy. Figures don't lie.

5

John R. Christy

Dr. John R. Christy is professor of atmospheric science and director of the Earth System Science Center at the University of Alabama in Huntsville, where he studies global climate issues. He and Dr. Roy W. Spencer were awarded NASA's Medal for Exceptional Scientific Achievement for developing a global temperature data set from microwave data observed from satellites. Dr. Christy has served as a contributor and lead author for the UN reports by the Intergovernmental Panel on Climate Change in which the satellite temperatures were included as a high-quality data set for studying global climate change.

WHAT A CLIMATOLOGIST CANNOT KNOW ABOUT THE NEXT 50 YEARS (BUT WHAT HE DOES BELIEVE)

What is it that a climatologist could possibly write in 2007 that would have any credibility fifty years from now? The climate system is so complicated and the crude predictive models used today are so inadequate that we simply do not have in hand confident forecasts to describe future changes in the types of weather people really care about.

I can *not* know whether there will be more or less rain (or snow) for any part of the planet. But I *believe* that as more sensible water policy evolves and the ingenuity of our engineers is brought to bear, more people will have access to more water than ever before.

I can *not* know the future levels of rivers and lakes. But I *believe* that these bodies of water will be cleaner and that the scourge of waterborne diseases, which today kill millions each year, will be addressed and dramatically reduced.

I can *not* know whether the temperature will be hotter or colder, though the sense today is that in most places the average temperature will be a bit warmer. However, I *believe* that more people will live and work in structures that protect them from the extremes of hot and cold that only the richer people of the world now enjoy. And I *believe* we shall be continually amazed at the resilience of the planet's living systems.

> *I can not know the extent of Arctic Sea ice in 2058. But I believe that there will be at least as many polar bears as there are today because they are exceptionally adaptive creatures.*

I can *not* know the extent of Arctic Sea ice in 2058. But I *believe* that there will be at least as many polar bears as there are today because they are exceptionally adaptive creatures and I suspect more regulatory action to limit hunting quotas will likely occur.

I can *not* know whether there will be more or fewer hurricanes, or whether they will be more or less intense, though research today indicates no noticeable changes in fifty years. I can only *hope*, however, that by 2058 sensible decisions will have been made to prevent vulnerable and expensive infrastructure from being built in harm's way on our active coastlines.

I can *not* know exactly how much higher sea level will be, though I suspect it will be about six inches as it continues its rise from the last ice age. But I *believe* this rise will not catch anyone off guard or be a significant problem.

I can *not* know what forms of power generation will be enhancing the lives of people in 2058. But I *believe* that energy production will grow considerably to meet the rising demand simply because the benefits of energy to human life are innumerable and ubiquitous. And, I *believe* that the millions of people now destroying natural habitats to gather biomass for burning will be liberated from this burden as modern power systems expand, thereby preserving the natural landscapes now being decimated.

I can *not* know what forms of governance will be operational among the nations in 2058, though my early experience as a missionary in Africa enlightened me as to the darker types. But I *believe* that the move toward democratically accountable systems will continue to be the key impetus for enhancing the quality of life for humans and everything else. I *believe* human rights will expand to include more women and children, and opportunity will flower among the nations.

In summary, I can *not* know what the trajectory of the climate system will be well enough to advise policy makers today on what specific course it will take, or well enough to help them know what they could possibly do to tweak it toward a direction deemed "safe," or even well enough to appear exceptionally prescient to those reading this in the future. But I *do believe* that the accumulating economic development throughout the world will not be sidetracked by calls to "stop global warming," which are ultimately designed to inhibit access to affordable energy. As a result, I *believe* more and more people will experience better health and security and that this will be accompanied by the additional bonus of a better-preserved natural environment.

In other words, I envy those in 2058, including my grandchildren who will then be about fifty-ish, living amidst the astounding advancements to come to pass, including the enhancements to both the environment and human prosperity now only a dream to billions.

6

Louis J. Ignarro

Louis J. Ignarro, PhD, is Distinguished Professor of Pharmacology at the UCLA School of Medicine. He and two other researchers received the Nobel Prize in Medicine in 1998 for their three major discoveries involving nitric oxide as a unique signaling molecule in the cardiovascular system. He is the author of NO More Heart Disease: How Nitric Oxide Can Prevent—Even Reverse—Heart Disease and Strokes.

NO MORE HEART DISEASE

Despite the dismal fact that cardiovascular disease is the leading cause of morbidity and untimely death in both men and women today, I am optimistic that we will experience a reversal of this world trend during the next fifty years. Cardiovascular disease is largely a lifestyle disease brought about gradually but with certainty by years of unhealthy dieting and a sedentary way of life. Only forty years ago, cardiovascular disease was considered to be a man's disease and women were thought to be largely protected, perhaps because of higher estrogen levels in the body. Instead, cancer was the number one killer of women. Today, however, this statistic has shifted in alarming fashion and more women than men die of cardiovascular disease each year. How and why did this tragedy occur in a world that is experiencing exponential advances in science and technology?

The current belief is that women have changed their lifestyles for the worse. Compare a typical woman living in the 1960s to a typical woman of today in Western countries. Their increased involvement in professional and non-professional jobs outside the home has fostered the development of dramatic changes in daily living habits not only for themselves but also for their families, especially their children. Women now spend much less time in the home preparing healthy meals for themselves and their families. What was once a healthy home-cooked meal has turned into a much less healthy, rapidly prepared meal or, worse yet, an unhealthy "fast food" meal. Coupled with a more sedentary lifestyle, poor dieting has led to an astonishing increase in the incidence of child, adolescent, and adult obesity in both males and females. The percentage of Americans that are considered to be morbidly obese is staggering, and the largest percentage increase is evident in children and adolescents. This trend is also apparent for the rest of the world population. When I walk around in any city in the United States or abroad, I am struck by the increasing number of morbidly obese children. The tragic consequence of this depressing trend has been an alarming rise in the incidence of diabetes, stroke, and heart attack. The medical community now understands that the starting point of most deaths due to cardiovascular disease is childhood obesity. This must be considered to be a very serious condition that will ultimately progress to metabolic disturbances and diabetes, which then sets the stage for cardiovascular disease. The point that I am trying to make is that cardiovascular disease is largely a preventable lifestyle disease. A change to a healthy lifestyle will markedly reduce the number of deaths attributed to cardiovascular disease.

The sad feature of this worsening trend is that it does not have to occur at all. If we would just improve our lifestyles, all of this might go away. I truly believe that through persistent increased public awareness, people will suddenly recognize that they are in control of their own destiny and that of their families. The result will be a much healthier population with a much lower incidence of cardiovascular disease. We can see today that significant change has already started to take place. For example, more and more people are paying attention to their diets and engaging in more exercise activities both indoors and outdoors. We can also see growing numbers of health food stores, attention to organically grown fruits and vegetables, healthier ingredients in canned and packaged foods, a wide array of healthy dietary supplements, and more and more books on the subject of healthy living. This demonstrates an increase in public awareness. But we need much more. People must increasingly be made aware that their fate and perhaps the fate of their family members rest largely on the decisions they make about lifestyle. I believe that the news media will soon recognize how important this is and respond in unique ways to improve public awareness of this serious problem. News media coverage of this problem is already underway with pertinent and convincing articles published in leading newspapers and magazines. But this kind of coverage must be enhanced and needs to be presented regularly on national radio and television. For example, programs devoted exclusively to adopting a healthy lifestyle should air widely and regularly.

Scientific evidence is overwhelming that foods containing saturated fats and trans fats can lead to cardiovascular problems. Similarly, a diet that is deficient in antioxidants can elicit the same problem. The reason for this is that excess saturated fats and inadequate antioxidants lead to a deficiency of nitric oxide (abbreviated NO) in the body. NO is a biological molecule that serves to protect us against cardiovascular disease, and a deficiency in NO will set the stage for serious cardiovascular disease such as coronary artery disease, stroke, and heart attack. Diets rich in protein, unsaturated fats, and antioxidants will increase the production and protective action of NO in the body. Similarly, exercise is well-known to accelerate NO production rapidly and effectively. Hence the phrase "exercise is good for your health." It is easy to see how and why a healthy diet together with adequate exercise can protect us against cardiovascular disease. The first word in the title of this essay, NO, signifies nitric oxide. Clearly, an unhealthy lifestyle can lead to cardiovascular disease and a significantly shorter life span. Many of my friends and my family have reacted to this knowledge by outlining, planning, and embarking on weight reduction programs, healthy diets at home and in restaurants, and moderate to extensive exercise programs. We have organized running, cycling, and swimming groups. Many of us have joined local sports clubs or fitness centers. Groups of us take vacations that involve not only healthy eating but also lots of physical activity such as walking, hiking, running, cycling, swimming, and playing tennis. This change in lifestyle feels great, makes everyone more trim, and is contagious in that it attracts more and more participants from both within and outside our local community.

We have recognized that the great majority of people who have decided to adopt a healthy lifestyle are well educated. This appears to be true also in other parts of the world and is not unexpected. More education generally means more wealth and perhaps more time to devote to healthy cooking and exercise. However, I believe that the less educated are also less informed, and herein lies the problem. We need to reach out and take our important message to all people, regardless of level of education or wealth. This can and will be accomplished not only by the news media but also by example. I am optimistic that people will experience a dramatic shift to a healthy lifestyle during the next fifty years.

7

E. Fuller Torrey

*Dr. E. Fuller Torrey is a research psychiatrist specializing in schizophrenia
and manic-depressive illness. Called "the most famous psychiatrist in America"
by the* Washington Post, *Dr. Torrey is president of the Treatment Advocacy
Center and is associate director for Laboratory Research at the Stanley
Medical Research Institute. Among his many awards are two commendation
medals from the US Public Health Service and a humanitarian award from
the National Alliance for Research on Schizophrenia and Depression.*

The End of Psychiatric Illnesses

Fifty years from now, I will not have a job. As a psychiatric researcher specializing in schizophrenia and bipolar disorder, there will be nothing to research,
since both diseases will be well understood and treatable. Most cases of these
diseases that we see today will, by then, be known to be caused by infectious
agents combined with predisposing genes; these cases will no longer be seen,
since children will be vaccinated against the infectious agents before they
become exposed. A small number of cases, caused by particular genetic com-
binations, brain injuries, and other insults to the brain, will still occur, but we
will have effective medications for treating such cases.

It will not only be schizophrenia and bipolar disorder that will have been
proven to be caused by infectious agents, but also Parkinson's disease,
Alzheimer's disease, multiple sclerosis, rheumatoid arthritis, and some cancers,

as well as other chronic diseases. What will surprise everyone will be the discovery that many of the infectious agents causing these diseases are being transmitted to humans from animals. Thus, fifty years from now, the relationship between humans and animals will be more distant. Dogs will still commonly be kept as pets, but keeping cats, hamsters, birds, and other animals will be uncommon because of the known danger of infectious agents they carry. Our fourteen-thousand-year-old relationship with dogs, by contrast, means that the infectious agents were transmitted to us long ago and are no longer pathogenic.

Dogs will still commonly be kept as pets, but keeping cats, hamsters, birds, and other animals will be uncommon because of the known danger of infectious agents they carry.

There will be other jobs for me, however, doing research on the brain. We will understand much more about how the modules of the brain function and the effect of genes and childhood experiences on human behavior, but there will still be much to learn. Looking back fifty years from now, our present knowledge of brain function will be similar to how phrenology looks to us today.

Our ability to better understand brain function will bring problems. One area of great interest will be our technological ability to read other people's minds. Utilizing neuroimaging techniques much more sensitive than anything now imaginable, we will, for example, have the ability to tell when people are not telling the truth. This will cause enormous ethical and legal problems involving the use of this technology. It will have a profound effect on criminal behavior and the law but will also affect things such as marital relations, statements by politicians and public officials, advertising, and claims by corporate executives for their products. People will wistfully recall the early days of the twenty-first century when people could still lie without fear of being subjected to a handheld brain scanner. Incidentally, the scanners will all be manufactured in Cambodia on contract from Chinese companies.

8

Arthur Caplan

Arthur Caplan is chair of the Department of Medical Ethics and director of the Center for Bioethics at the University of Pennsylvania. He writes a column on bioethics for MSNBC.com and is a frequent commentator on various media outlets. He is the author of Smart Mice, Not So Smart People: An Interesting and Amusing Guide to Bioethics *and* Who Owns Life?

Simon Caplan's Day

Simon Caplan finished his breakfast of genetically engineered juice designed for his specific genotype; toast made, in part, from the secretions of microbes growing healthy fiber in the temperature-controlled vats at the local green farm; and scrambled eggs from chickens cloned to produce low-cholesterol, high-protein eggs. He had a busy day ahead.

In addition to his doctor's appointment, he was scheduled to spend the afternoon on his work computer inputting data and responding to the information sent from his colleagues in China and India about weather control. Simon is a climate engineer—he works for a huge international consortium involved in keeping the earth's atmosphere clean and maximally safe for its human inhabitants, their pets, and the few wild animal species left in zoos, clonariums, and aquatic preserves.

Simon knew he had a long day ahead of him. It was tough being expected to work five hours a day. He thought he had better take twice the normal dose of his cognitive enhancement supplement—after all, what could it hurt? Then he remembered he would be checking in with the doctor via his telediagnostic box and that double-dose would surely show up on the telemetry toxicology screen. That would mean a fine, since it had recently been agreed as a condition of his climate job that no employer could require taking more than one cognitive enhancer per day. Swallowing that extra pill meant a mandatory counseling tape in his virtual reality system plus some online classroom time with the human egalitarian relations department—something he did not have time for right now. One pill would have to do.

Simon was antsy. Nothing a mood stabilizer could not handle, but he knew the reason for his anxiety. His test results were coming back soon from the National Genetics Authority about whether he could marry his girlfriend, Suzy. He did not have the best of genotypes, but Suzy—Suzy was incredible. Still, without the approval of the NGA, they would not have government approval to marry and have kids. If they did anyway that would mean they would be facing an enormous tax burden for any sick or disabled children they had.

Things sure had gotten complicated living in the North American Alliance. As he logged on he found his mind drifting back to memories he had from talking with his dad about a simpler time fifty years earlier when people actually went to work, had personal contact with a doctor, and could marry without worrying about the genetic consequences of reproduction. *Still,* he thought, *I have it better than my grandfather, Art. He died, frail and decrepit, at the relatively young age of eighty.* Simon could look forward to a minimum of 140 years of high-quality life with at least half of that spent in retirement pursuing his hobbies, time in the virtual reality pleasure center, or socially useful volunteer work. *Seems a small price to pay,* he thought—*my life is designed, engineered, and shaped by all manner of technology.* Not a lot of choice in that, but what would you choose—a life twice as long and twice as pleasant as your grandparents or one sitting in cars in polluted air eating food from sick and diseased plants and animals, struggling to travel twenty miles so you could work nine hours? *No contest,* he thought.

9

Wanda Jones

Dr. Wanda Jones is the director of the Office on Women's Health at the U.S. Department of Health and Human Services, where she oversees ten areas of women's health, including HIV/AIDS, cardiovascular disease, violence against women, diabetes and obesity, lupus, breastfeeding, and mental health. She was previously at the Centers for Disease Control, where she was active in policy issues related to HIV laboratory testing, women and AIDS, HIV vaccine development, and healthcare workers.

FIFTY YEARS FROM NOW: TODAY'S BABY REACHES MIDDLE AGE

Imagine the future headlines:

2058: Persons aged 50–70 more disabled than their parents

If today's trends in weight gain and obesity among children in the United States continue, in 50 years the adults they become will be marked by limitations in daily activities (mobility, household and personal care tasks) that today characterize many people over age 80. Arthritis, diabetes, heart disease, and cancers are the major health consequences of obesity; risk is increased when a person is even moderately overweight. The prevalence of these diseases historically has increased at midlife, but public health began sounding the alarm about diabetes increasing among children and young adults a decade ago. Our continued deafness to the calls for lifestyle changes bodes poorly.

2058: *Workforce Opportunities for Persons 70 and Older*

By 2058 the United States will experience a shift in workforce demographics. The Census Bureau forecasts that the population of peak working-age adults, ages 25–44, will be smaller than it was during World War II. The echo boomers—children of the baby boomers—will be 45 and older and likely will be working into their 70s, partly because of the labor shortage, but also because they can. Those with the most options for changing jobs and recasting their careers will have escaped the perils of obesity. These workers won't stay at the same jobs; in fact, they may have several careers, with many more options available after age 60 than even we had imagined.

2058: *Life expectancy declines after 30-year stagnation*

A girl born today can expect to live nearly 81 years, a boy, almost 76. Life expectancy is calculated from death rates at various ages across the population. Populations that experience high infant, child, and young adult mortality rates generally have lower life expectancies. The scary feature of any prediction about the U.S. population 50 years hence is the rising prevalence of diabetes, driven by exponential increases since the 1960s in excess weight gain and obesity among young people. That factor alone could reduce life expectancy by 3–5 years if we fail to address this threat to health security.

Where did we go wrong? Our mothers told us to eat right, get enough sleep, go out and play, and to be careful, but we seem to have quit listening. By the end of the twentieth century, U.S. health data showed accelerating trends in overweight, obesity, and sedentary activity dating to the 1960s. Baby boomers (born between 1946 and 1964) have seized advances in technology that allow us to travel from our armchairs, eat from our cars, and "live large" in ways our parents never imagined. Our children and grandchildren have only amplified these trends, with the generations following us living and socializing electronically in ways *we* never imagined. Their world at midlife will be vastly changed from what we take for granted now.

Technology has given us many things, reducing the amount of physical effort we expend in daily activities. At the same time, for most Americans, food has never been more abundant and easier to obtain, and these two trends have contributed to our weight problem.

One of the criticisms of technology is that it isolates people from face-to-face social interaction. I believe the next 50 years will bring technologic touch—the neural impulses that allow us to feel, smell, and taste. This alone will change electronic shopping (some of us just have to feel the heft or softness or texture of something we might like to buy) and entertainment (the virtual getaway), but it will have far more significant implications for the delivery of health care and preventive medicine. Office visits may become a thing of the past, if a provider can conduct a complete history and physical over the internet. New imaging devices—small, powerful, and relatively inexpensive—will assist with previously invasive or intrusive exams. Only rarely will a physical specimen (blood, urine, or tissue) need to be obtained, and that will be limited to advanced-care settings (successors to hospitals).

Genetic profiles at birth (perhaps before) will be routine. Gene therapy will be able to correct many defects that shorten life or reduce quality of life, and support structures will be in place to help families and individuals control modifiable risk factors (that may or may not interact with genetics to cause disease). Many organs and tissues will be manufactured, either from sophisticated materials or from a recipient's own cells, eliminating the risk of rejection.

Smoking will be almost unheard of, but other addictions will evolve and require attention (such is the nature of humans, but these biochemical pathways will be better understood and amenable to various treatments as well). All but a few types of breast and prostate cancers will be curable. Several cancers (stomach, pancreas) and autoimmune diseases (multiple sclerosis, myasthenia gravis) will have a vaccine to prevent them. The blood-brain barrier will fall, and mental and physical health will be fully integrated and encompassed in all health disciplines. Alzheimer's will be preventable and treatable (although not yet curable).

Health will be thought of as a global investment, not a national or corporate venture. Technology will perfect and secure the electronic health record, and any indicated interventions (preventive, diagnostic, and curative) will be automatically prompted, recorded, and monitored by the electronic health record. Each individual will have direct access to his or her own records via a pocket-sized device,

> *Health will be thought of as a global investment, not a national or corporate venture.*

which will record physiologic and other data about the wearer's activities, diet, emotional state, and other components to aid in risk assessment. That device may also deliver treatment and provide ongoing monitoring for some physical and mental illnesses. Implantable and patchlike devices will be commonplace for those with chronic conditions; they will deliver medicine or directly modify biochemical pathways by influencing defective enzymatic or other processes. Furthermore, we will better understand how physiology changes over the lifespan, and how it differs between the sexes and among populations (as well as at the individual level). This will result in even more efficient and effective preventive, medical, and mental health services.

Because no one lives forever, society will be better equipped to deal humanely with end of life issues. Health-care professionals will have tools for assessing futility of treatment and better ways of easing pain of terminal illnesses. Family support will allow loved ones to stay engaged (even from a distance) at this final transition. Far-improved systems of home- and community-based care will allow the aged and disabled to stay in their homes as long as they choose, rather than being forced into long-term care or other dependent living.

Broad alliances between employers, education systems (all types and ages), faith groups, and communities will help identify families and youths at risk, providing wraparound services to support literacy and skills development.

Direct intervention will reduce diabetes, reduce family and community violence, improve mental health, and reduce underemployment.

Extended life spans will create new opportunities in education, workforce, and leisure. Technologic advances will allow almost anyone who wants to work to do so, with options for working from home, assistive technologies, and knowledge-based employment that is less physically demanding. Education may be interrupted by a period of service between high school and college, allowing young people to explore fields for which they have aptitude but no previous exposure. And periods of work may be interrupted by periods of education, particularly allowing mid-life and older workers to learn new skills for second or third careers. Lifelong learning will be a national mantra.

I can't even address who pays. With tremendous pressures by baby boomer retirements and increasing consequences of being overweight or obese among Medicaid populations, it's not clear that Medicare and Medicaid or even private insurance as we know it now can survive without significant changes. Reframing health as wellness first—instead of medical care—will open new opportunities by applying a range of technologies to assess individuals, families, and communities for optimal lifestyle strategies, and provide the necessary support to achieve them.

Massive change over the next 50 years will happen, and we must drive it, unless we are willing to accept the increased disability and reduced life expectancy consequences of the poor choices being made today.

I hope to be among the several million centenarians 50 years from now, by doing all I can to control the risks I know I have. The choices I make every day about my diet, my activity, my safety, and so many others will stack the odds for me. I'm excited about even having the possibility of being here in 2058! Besides, by then I'm confident I can put my feet up and read the stack of books I have no time for now. Even if technology allows us to literally "absorb" knowledge in 50 years, nothing beats the satisfaction of turning the last page in a good book.

10

Craig Newmark

Craig Newmark is an Internet pioneer and founder of craigslist, the community bulletin board of the Internet.

BLOGGING FROM THE FUTURE

Those kids, they don't know how good it is these days. When I first used systems, I had to make my own bits. (Seriously speaking, I used punch cards.)

Now we all take intimate, ubiquitous computing for granted. Some of us prefer implants; some prefer using contact lenses as very wide-screen displays. It's all wireless, often powered by our own body movement. Some of us are in love with the technology, including myself, but what this all is about is the way people use the tech to help their living.

People forgot that the 'net was invented about five hundred years ago by this guy, Johannes Gutenberg. However, his tech languished for a while until an early blogger, Martin Luther, invented the first killer ap, the Reformation.

People used this technology to redistribute power, from smaller groups to larger (less small) groups. Notable among 'em were John Locke, a blogger associated with the British Revolution of 1688. Later on we have Thomas Paine and the American Revolution of 1776.

It took a lot more bloggers to restore the American Constitution in 2008. People forget that a tipping point occurred that year; citizen journalists exposed so much corruption that the mainstream press followed through. That was the real beginning of continuous coverage of governance via Congresspedia. Until 2008, the victors, the guys with guns, wrote what we'd consider history. That year, the history of record became Wikipedia.

What I think happened is that the mass of humanity, who are almost all moderates, got tired of the fanatics, got connected via the 'net, and started to run things. Like Jon Stewart said, used to be that the extremists got lots of attention, because the moderates have stuff to do.

That's how moderate Palestinians and Israelis got peace; they took control of the peace process via the OneVoice thing, and made a deal.

Me, I gotta go. Running late for my telomere treatment, which keeps me looking fifty though I'm twice that.

You kids! Get off my lawn!

11

Ray Kurzweil

Ray Kurzweil is an inventor whose developments include the first print-to-speech reading machine for the blind and the first text-to-speech synthesizer. He was inducted into the National Inventors Hall of Fame and is the recipient of the Lemelson-MIT Prize, the nation's largest award in invention and innovation, and the National Medal of Technology, the nation's highest honor in technology. His latest book is The Singularity Is Near: When Humans Transcend Biology.

PROGRESS ACCELERATES EXPONENTIALLY

"You can't predict the future" is the common wisdom. Indeed, this aphorism is true for specific projects. But the overall progression of information technologies is remarkably predictable. The price-performance of computing has grown at a remarkably smooth, doubly exponential pace for over a century, going back to the data processing equipment used in the 1890 US census. Events such as two world wars, the Cold War, the Great Depression, all kinds of good times and bad did not register at all on what was an inevitable progression.

This observation, what I call "the law of accelerating returns," is not limited to electronic devices but applies to any area of technology in which we can measure the information content. As just a few of many examples, the cost of genetic sequencing has come down by half every year, from $10 per base pair in 1990 to a fraction of a penny today. The spatial resolution of brain scanning has become twice as precise (in 3D volume) every year, while the amount of brain data has doubled each year. Performance of communication technologies including the Internet—measured in many different ways—has also doubled about every year.

The result of this exponential progression of information technology is an acceleration in the rate of progress itself, which according to my model is now doubling every decade. While this may seem obvious, it is remarkable how often otherwise thoughtful observers fail to take this into consideration. The last time I participated in a project in which we were asked to look fifty years into the future was a 2003 conference organized by *Time* magazine called "The Future of Life," on the occasion of the fiftieth anniversary of the discovery of the structure of DNA. All of the speakers at the conference, except for myself and one other speaker (Bill Joy), used the last fifty years as a model for the next half century. This included James Watson, the DNA co-discoverer, who predicted that in fifty years we'll have drugs that enable you to eat as much as you want without gaining weight. I replied, "Jim, we've already demonstrated that in animals by blocking the fat insulin receptor gene, and there are several pharmaceutical companies rushing to bring this insight to the human market. We'll see that in one decade, not five."

As prodigious and influential as information technology is already, we'll see a billionfold improvement in the next quarter century, and then we'll see it again.

In a similar manner, almost all of the predictions were dramatically understated by failing to take the exponential nature of technological progress into consideration. I believe that this is hardwired: our brains were designed by evolution to make linear predictions, which work well when you're trying to predict the path of a predator scampering toward you. But this linear thinking is ill suited for long-term predictions.

Doubling the price-performance, capacity, and bandwidth of information technologies in under a year represents an extraordinary progression: an improvement of over a thousand in a decade, a factor of a billion in twenty-five years. When I came to MIT, the university had one computer shared by thousands of faculty and students. It took up the floor of a large building and cost well over $10 million. Today, the computer in your $50 cell phone is thousands of times more powerful. As prodigious and influential as information technology is already, we'll see a billionfold improvement in the next quarter century, and then we'll see it again.

This is not just "Moore's Law" (the shrinking of components on a flat integrated circuit). When that paradigm runs out of steam before 2020, we'll go to another paradigm: three-dimensional circuits made of self-organizing molecules, which will continue the exponential progression well into the twenty-first century. We are also shrinking technology, both electronic and mechanical, at a rate of over 100 per 3D volume per decade, which translates into a 100,000-fold decrease in size in the next quarter century.

This extraordinary progression is not limited to computers and electronics but will ultimately transform every aspect of our lives. Biology and medicine, for example, used to be hit or miss, happening to find chemicals that had some benefit but invariably included many side effects and drawbacks. We are now beginning to understand and simulate biology as the set of information processes that it truly represents. And we are gaining the tools to reprogram those processes. We have outdated software running in our bodies: our twenty-three thousand genes evolved when conditions were very different. For example, it was not in the interest of our species for people to live past childrearing. Once you were done raising your kids—which was the case when you were in your mid-twenties and your kids were young teens—you were just using up the very limited resources of the clan. So a thousand years ago, human life expectancy was twenty-five. It was only thirty-seven as recently as two hundred years ago.

We now have the means to turn genes off (with a technology called RNA interference), and to add new genes using new reliable forms of gene therapy. A company I help direct takes lung cells out of the body, adds a new gene in a

Petri dish, inspects that the new gene was correctly inserted, replicates the cell a millionfold, and then injects the gene-modified cells back into the body, where they end up back in the lungs. This has cured pulmonary hypertension, a fatal disease, and is now undergoing human trials. We are headed not just for designer babies but designer baby boomers (something I'm personally more interested in).

We are headed not just for designer babies but designer baby boomers (something I'm personally more interested in).

Human life expectancy has doubled in the last two centuries, and the rate of increase will soon go into high gear. In a decade, biotechnology will be a thousand times more powerful than it is today. In about fifteen years, according to my models, we'll be adding more than a year each year to your remaining life expectancy. That will not represent a guarantee of eternal life, but it will represent a tipping point.

A concern often sparked by this observation is that we will run out of resources such as energy. But information technology will transform these areas as well. A revolution overlapping the reprogramming of biology is nanotechnology, a technology in which key features are only a few billionths of a meter. We are rapidly moving toward an era in which we can essentially program matter and energy at the molecular level to create almost any physical product we need at extremely low cost.

Today, you can turn an information file into a sound recording, or a movie, or a book. In a couple of decades, you will be able to turn information files into a wide range of physical products and "print" them out with an inexpensive tabletop molecular "nanofactory." So you will be able to e-mail a toaster, or even the toast. One of the products we will "print" out will be highly efficient, lightweight, and inexpensive solar panels. We are awash in sunlight: we only need to capture 1 part in 10,000 of the sunlight that falls on the earth (this will rise to 3 parts in 10,000 by 2025) to meet 100 percent of our energy needs. This will be easy and inexpensive to do in twenty years using nanoengineered solar panels. We will store the energy in tiny, massively distributed nanoengineered fuel cells.

The most daunting implication of this inexorable progression of information technology will be the reverse-engineering and resulting amplification of human intelligence itself. We have already modeled and simulated twenty regions of the human brain, including regions of the auditory cortex, the visual cortex, and the Cerebellum (responsible for skill formation). An ambitious simulation of the cerebral cortex (responsible for abstract reasoning) is already underway at IBM. I've made the case that we will have detailed models and simulations of all several hundred regions of the human brain within about twenty years, and we will be able to run these simulations on inexpensive computers that will exceed the computational capacity of the human brain.

The implications will be several-fold. We will gain far greater insight into human nature, which has been a primary goal of the arts and sciences since our species started those evolutionary processes. We will be in a far superior position to fix problems that arise in the human brain. Most importantly, we will expand the artificial intelligence (AI) tool kit. Already today, AI programs perform hundreds of tasks that used to be performed by humans. These are deeply embedded in our modern infrastructure and include such varied tasks as diagnosing electrocardiograms and medical images, automatically detecting financial fraud, making billions of dollars of daily investment decisions, designing products, maintaining just-in-time inventory levels, assembling products in automated factories, guiding intelligent weapons, and a myriad of others. The depth and breadth of these intelligent algorithms is growing and within a quarter century will rival the full range of human intelligence. Combining the types of intelligence that humans now excel in (principally our ability to recognize patterns) with ways in which machines have traditionally been superior (such as sharing knowledge at electronic speeds) will be formidable.

In my view, creating a new intelligent "species" is not the primary implication of creating human-level AI. Rather we will merge with the intelligent technology that we are creating. We are already placing intelligent devices in our bodies and brains. Parkinson's patients can replace the brain tissue destroyed by the disease with a pea-sized computer placed in their brains. The latest generation of this FDA-approved neural implant allows patients to update the software in the computer in their brains from outside their bodies. We already have experimental blood-cell-sized devices that carry out sophisticated functions such as finding and destroying cancer cells inside the bloodstream. In twenty years, these "nanobots" in the bloodstream will be keeping us healthy from inside. They will go inside our brains noninvasively through the capillaries and interact with our biological neurons. Billions of distributed nanobots in the brain will provide full-immersion virtual reality experiences from inside the nervous system as well as augmented reality. Most importantly, we will directly expand our memories, pattern-recognition capabilities, cognitive faculties, and every aspect of our intelligence.

Will these computers inside our brains just be tools like today's pocket computers that we place inside our brains because that will be a convenient place to put them? Or will we consider these brain extenders to be part of ourselves? I've asked Parkinson's patients whether they regard the computer inside their heads as part of themselves. Almost all such patients respond that they consider the implants to be part of who they are. I get the same reply from deaf persons with cochlear implants. I expect that we will feel the same way about the nanobots that will be widely distributed though our bodies and brains.

Because of the law of accelerating returns, the nonbiological portion of our intelligence will grow exponentially, whereas the biological portion will remain effectively fixed. In light of this, will we remain human? The answer depends on how you define the term. If you define *human* as characterized by our current limitations, then the answer is no. In my view, defining our human identity in terms of old restrictions is an essentially fundamentalist position. We are the only species that seeks—and succeeds—in soaring past our boundaries. From that perspective, we will just be continuing an old story of accelerating progress.

12

Thomas C. Schelling

Thomas C. Schelling, Distinguished University Professor at the University of Maryland School of Public Policy, shared the Nobel Prize in Economics in 2005 for having enhanced our understanding of conflict and cooperation through game-theory analysis. Other honors include the National Academy of Sciences Award for Behavioral Research Relevant to the Prevention of Nuclear War.

AN ECONOMIST PREDICTS

Nuclear weapons have gone unused for more than eleven decades. France and the United Kingdom have abandoned their nuclear forces. Iran and North Korea have acquired nuclear weapons but have since disposed of them, along with India and Pakistan (but not Israel). No other nations beyond the United States, Russia, and China are currently known to possess nuclear weapons.

Terrorist actions, both domestic and international, continue at about the level experienced fifty years ago but have ceased to be the overriding preoccupation that they used to be. On the fiftieth anniversary of 9/11, more than five billion people watched video of the Twin Trade Towers attack of 2001. There is continuing concern that some terrorist organization may acquire nuclear weapons; none is yet known to possess them, none having claimed possession. Biological weapons are still a concern; no contagious outbreak has yet been attributed to deliberate infection.

The advent of global warming resulting from human activity has been identified beyond question. None of the earlier dire prediction has been realized, but the concentration of greenhouse gases in the atmosphere continues to increase. Water shortage in much of the world, though not entirely due to climate change, has been aggravated by the global warming. International cooperation to abate emissions is still without agreed obligations; three-quarters of all nations are unengaged, and scientists predict severe consequences.

No large-scale introduction of new, non-fossil energy sources has yet occurred nor is imminently expected. Capture and underground storage of CO_2 is still in the exploratory stage; exploitation of undersea methane deposits is being explored. Proposals to put reflecting substances in the stratosphere or in orbit to reflect as much as 1 percent of incoming sunlight, to offset the "greenhouse effect," is both attracting scientific attention and detracting from the motivation to abate emissions on the scale required.

Several, but not all, of the worst contagious diseases, especially vector-borne tropical diseases (including malaria), have been eradicated or brought under control. Thus some of the worst expected consequences of global warming are greatly diminished. Rising standards of nutrition and maternal and child health care, together with better drinking water and sewage disposal and greatly developed public health infrastructure, have further diminished the severity of infectious diseases in the developing world, large parts of which, including China and India, have progressed dramatically.

Russia, except for its nuclear arsenal, is not the superpower that fifty years ago it was expected to be; its economy has not kept up with most of the world's, its scientific and literary achievements have been disappointing, and its population has been declining. In contrast, the United States continues to be the world's leader in science, technology, and innovation, and has long since recovered its status—subdued and diminished early in the century—as the world's model of democracy and international cooperation.

Technologically the world is much as it was back in the early 2000s. A middle-class American child, if transported back fifty years to a similar household, would find little to puzzle over and not much to miss.

World population appears to have stabilized at about 8.5 billion. Immigration has kept the most developed countries from too severe a decline in population. Lifetimes have continued to increase throughout the world, especially now that AIDS has been eliminated, but the appearance of elderliness, anticipated fifty years ago, is masked by the extension of good health and vitality, and, in the more developed world, surgical, prosthetic, and medical advances that have greatly reduced many disabilities that used to be so conspicuous. Alzheimer's, unfortunately, is still with us.

In contrast to half a century ago, the White House is occupied by the second woman president; three of the nine Supreme Court justices are women; eleven state governors are women, and the chairman of the Joint Chiefs of Staff, a general of the army, is a woman. A woman astronaut is commander of the small but burgeoning US observatory and space station on the Moon, which is beginning to resemble the Antarctica of a century ago.

The Islamic world is still struggling with modernity, but the struggle does not inhibit young people in large numbers from studying in China, India, Japan, the United States, and Europe. The recent award of Nobel Prizes in medicine and economics to Muslims has aroused pride and strengthened ties with the Western intellectual community.

The use of tobacco, which peaked worldwide twenty years ago after rising incomes made cigarettes affordable and "liberated" women from inhibition, is beginning to decline as more and more governments in the developing world follow those of most developed nations in discouraging smoking or even prohibiting it in some jurisdictions. The use of addictive drugs has increased in the past fifty years, despite successful development of some potent medicinal inhibitors,

> *In contrast to half a century ago, the White House is occupied by the second woman president; three of the nine Supreme Court justices are women; eleven state governors are women, and the chairman of the Joint Chiefs of Staff, a general of the army, is a woman.*

but most nations gave up (or in the developing world never launched) the "war" on drugs, and neither the use nor the traffic is the scourge that it had been in some of the developed world.

It is now three years since the state of Israel has been mentioned on the front page of the *New York Times*. The prime minister of Israel was planning to issue a happy comment but desisted for fear it would be featured on the front page of the *New York Times*.

13

Chandrasekhar (Spike) Narayan

Spike Narayan holds a PhD in materials science and has been with IBM's Research Division for over twenty years. His research interests are primarily in the area of materials and process technologies relevant to the semiconductor industry, and he has extensive experience in science and technology at the nanoscale.

DIARY ENTRY: 2058

On this cool March morning (year 2058) in northern California, I was gently awakened by the alarm clock. I glanced at the time and noted it was a full hour earlier than usual. On the well-lit 25 cm screen (yes, the United States finally completed the switch to the metric system only five years ago!), there was a reminder about an early morning meeting I had to connect into to speak with my colleagues halfway around the world before they headed home for the evening. The truly interconnected home is finally a reality, and most of the early bugs have been ironed out a few years ago. My calendar automatically communicates my first appointment for the day to my alarm clock so I always have enough time to get ready. The alarm clock had already signaled the coffee pot to turn on, also an hour earlier than usual, and I could smell the aroma. As I walked to the kitchen, I recalled the days when people would step out to pick up the newspaper from their front yards. The age of the flexible displays has now completely taken over the news media business. Interestingly enough, the newspaper format has not changed. The flexible display is much like an old-fashioned newspaper in size and feel, except its content is automatically updated wirelessly every morning from the "home command hub." As I got ready and headed to the garage, I couldn't help noting that the grand city growth plans about mass transport hubs and housing developments clustered around them never really took off. This, I am sure, could be directly attributed to the fact that rapid developments in hybrid hydrogen/electric cars have greatly changed the energy consumption landscape and that solar cells on house rooftops have exceeded the 30 percent efficiency needed to make the average home reasonably energy self-sufficient.

On my way to meet with customers to see their research facility, I tuned in to an Indian radio station because I wanted to know the reactions to the press release about a new personalized cancer drug that was announced by a small pharmaceutical start-up in Chennai. The mass hysteria over carbon footprint forty years ago has shifted to genetic footprint for tailored drugs. While gene therapy is only now starting to show promise after several false starts, the area of personalized medicine has made great strides. Identifying the classes of effective drugs and dosages specific to individuals is now normal, and the genetic makeup of each child is determined within the first year of life so pediatricians can establish treatment patterns early in life.

My train of thought was rudely interrupted by a series of beeps from my car's navigation screen warning me that my usual route had some traffic problems and that I should pick one of the suggested alternate routes, which I did, and arrived at my client site on time. The truly connected sensor networks are now par for the course on most roadways. It must be noted that the vast majority of Americans have been telecommuting for the past two decades and a typical work group is globally distributed. The concept of driving to work has, for the most part, become a thing of the past. The trend greatly accelerated when most of the manufacturing activity migrated to the African continent, and the local economy of the North American continent was dominated by the service industry much like that of the European and Asian economies.

After my client visit, I got into my car, noticed on the screen that my wife's car was not too far from our favorite restaurant, and asked if she wanted to break for lunch. I got a positive response and headed to my lunch date. After a traditional hot meal, I glanced at my Terapod, a truly integrated handheld mobile device now quite ubiquitous, and noticed a change in my afternoon appointment. These devices are connected to high-speed wireless networks 24/7 and always have real-time information. As I pulled out of the restaurant, I noticed on the navigator screen that our two kids were on their way home from school with their Terapods faithfully transmitting their positions to the network.

The vast majority of Americans have been telecommuting for the past two decades and a typical work group is globally distributed. The concept of driving to work has, for the most part, become a thing of the past.

Later that evening after dinner we watched some personalized TV. Gone are the days of broadcast TV. Shows are now "published" directly into vast datacenters, and customers typically scan the databases to view shows of their choice at a time of their choice. Much of it has been enabled by storage becoming incredibly inexpensive. Abundant storage has completely altered our view of selecting and storing information. After watching their favorite shows, the kids wrapped up their group homework project. The truly massively parallel multi-person connectivity has changed the nature of working in groups, and schools are effectively using this medium to encourage peer-to-peer collaboration.

As we turned in for the night, I noticed my Terapod blinking, wrapping up our vacation plans for a trip overseas. It must have noticed a block of time convenient for the whole family and found a great deal and initiated the travel plans to a destination on our prioritized list. I wondered what it had picked. As I started to doze off, I reminded myself to check tomorrow morning to see where we are going for our holiday.

14

James E. Cartwright

General James E. Cartwright is commander of United States Strategic Command, Offutt Air Force Base, Nebraska. He is responsible for the global command and control of US strategic forces to meet decisive national security objectives. USSTRATCOM provides a broad range of strategic capabilities and options for the president and secretary of defense.

"There is not the slightest indication that nuclear energy will ever be obtainable. It would mean that the atom would have to be shattered at will."[1]

— *Albert Einstein, 1932*

DECIPHERING THE MEGA-TRENDS

Predicting the future is a formidable challenge, even for our best and brightest. Most of our predictions fail to intersect a future reality because, in order to be accurate, we must do more than extend familiar, observed trends and patterns into tomorrow. Military leaders are particularly susceptible to this phenomenon. We call it "fighting the last war." While familiar trends and patterns do aid our effort, it is often the *unexpected* developments, the *unforeseen* occurrences that are the drivers of history. The terrorist attacks of 9/11, the collapse of the USSR, the invention of the transistor and subsequently the microprocessor, the development of nuclear technology, the American Revolution, and the birth of the modern Nation-State at the conclusion of Europe's Thirty Years' War are all examples of events that were very difficult to forecast but did much to shape the world in which we now live. Unfortunately for the futurist, the interaction of events produces a complexity that does not easily lend itself to "preemptive" deciphering. I will, nevertheless, attempt the impossible.

There are two "mega-trends" that will likely shape the course of the next fifty years: continued changes in world population and demographics, and the advance of modern technology.

Although the rate of world population growth will slow, total world population will continue to grow. World population was a little less than 3 billion people in 1957, is approximately 6.5 billion today, and conservative estimates place it at 9–10 billion in 2058.[2] The bulk of this growth will occur in the littoral regions of the third world, predominantly in an area oftentimes referred to as the "Arc of Instability" (Central and South America, Africa, the Middle East, Central and Southeast Asia).[3] Population growth will be the result of both relatively high birth rates in the third world and longer life spans in countries with relatively lower birth rates, i.e., the United States, Canada, Japan, and Western Europe.[4] Thus, the people of today's Western industrialized world will comprise a much smaller portion of the world's population in 2058, and their median age will be much higher.

Population growth will increase the competition for natural resources, food, and living space. If mismanaged, it will increase the levels of pollution, poverty, and political and economic instability. Dramatically changing demographics will concentrate more population in the "Arc of Instability," the home of many of our allies, but also many of our enemies in the Global War on Terrorism. Capital

Capital flows and economic growth will be less concentrated in the West. China and India will likely be peer competitors, if not outright world economic leaders.

flows and economic growth will be less concentrated in the West. China and India will likely be peer competitors, if not outright world economic leaders.

Robert Fulton's steam engine and Eli Whitney's cotton gin were to the industrial age what William Shockley's transistor and Intel's microprocessor have been to the information age—catalysts that precipitated periods of rapid technological advance in historically short periods of time. In 1964, Gordon Moore postulated that the number of transistors able to be added to a microchip would double (and so, too, would computing power) every two years. Today that number doubles every eighteen months. This rapid increase in computing power has facilitated remarkable advances in every field of human endeavor: for industry, robotics and more efficient mass production; for agriculture, satellite-based land-use studies and genetic engineering advances in crops and livestock; for medicine, the mapping of the human genome; for the social sciences, the ability to more accurately measure and catalog our needs, desires, and motivations; for warfare, net-centric operations and stand-off precision; and *for all of us, the nearly instantaneous free flow of information through cyberspace connecting people throughout the world.*

This advance of technology will accelerate over the next fifty years. Over 80 percent of all scientists that have ever lived are alive today.[5] Both private and public research budgets continue to grow. By 2058, it is safe to say that the microprocessor (or whatever replaces it), regardless of whether Moore's Law holds, will be thousands, if not hundreds of thousands of times, more capable than today. This ever-increasing computing power, wielded by more and more highly trained scientists, doctors, entrepreneurs, students, and everyday citizens via the Internet and other media will contribute to society in a myriad of ways. The world will be replete with "complex adaptive systems," agents that consist of many individual, interacting parts that learn, change, adapt, and evolve themselves as they interact (such as the human immune system and the stock market).[6] Today's "change" will become tomorrow's "hyperchange."

As a result, the pace of globalization, which Thomas Friedman defines generally in his book *The World Is Flat* as the process of utilizing the mobility of information and capital to seek international economies of scale, will accelerate.[7]

Enabled by technological advances, and spurred by a growing population seeking scarce resources, global interdependence—economic, political, and social—will be the trademark of the new century. The currency of power will be information and knowledge. This power will be distributed across people, time, and geography. Information will move to the user, rather than the user moving to the information. As a result, individuals will be more empowered than ever, dramatically increasing creativity, productivity, and uncertainty, but also opportunity. Uncertainty will demand organizational flexibility to take advantage of opportunity.

Mankind's central organizing construct for the last 350 years has been the Nation-State. The Treaty of Westphalia codified the tenets of territorial sovereignty, political self-determination, secularized governments, and a recognized system of international relations. Hierarchal by design, fueled by nationalism, and designed to provide stability by leveraging the collective efforts of its citizens, Nation-State governments concentrate power based on a system of laws that oftentimes is very resistant to change.

The information age has eroded the powers of the Nation-State. It has facilitated the free flow of people, capital, and information across borders. This *mobility* has led to the formation of international trade organizations and agreements, the rise of multinational corporations, and the trend toward "supernational" political bodies such as the United Nations and the European Union, and other non-state actors. National currencies, symbolic of the economic power of the Nation-State, have begun to give way to common international currencies. Traditional alliances between Nation-States struggle to remain relevant.

Although Nation-States will continue to be challenged by the advance of technology, and weaker Nation-States may fracture, they will not disappear. They will be forced to adapt to accelerated change. In particular, they will have to learn to deal with non-state actors, "intermediate" entities that don't have a large infrastructure but do have the power, credibility, and authority to act in many ways like a Nation-State, or to influence Nation-States. From twentieth-century Nation-State threats we will see a transition to twenty-first-century decentralized networked threats from non-state enemies that will seek asymmetric advantage. Leveraging the tools of technology so readily available to us, our enemies will seek to beat us at our own game. They will be able to change, react, and mutate in minutes and hours, not days, weeks, months, or years. They will use the Internet, or whatever replaces the Internet, for "strategic communication." They will be able to readily examine our centers of gravity, identify our critical vulnerabilities, and devise methods to attack us.

Leveraging the tools of technology so readily available to us, our enemies will seek to beat us at our own game. They will be able to change, react, and mutate in minutes and hours, not days, weeks, months, or years.

The Nation-State will not be alone in this struggle. Other traditional organizational structures, designed during the industrial age to provide stability by gaining and maintaining advantage, will be challenged as well. In order to survive, organizations will become more decentralized, distributed, "flat," collaborative, integrated, and diverse. Society will be as "horizontally" oriented in 2058 as it is "vertically" oriented today. Able to more quickly adapt to change, smaller, decentralized organizations will have distinct advantages, or "reverse economies of scale," over traditional large, hierarchal organizations with slower decision cycles. They will look much more like starfish (a term given to decentralized, adaptable organizations by Ori Brafman and Rod A. Jackson in their book entitled *The Starfish and the Spider*) than spiders (centralized, hierarchal organizations).[8] Bureaucracies will be flattened and efficiencies gained by conducting distributed and disaggregated activities that can "swarm" or come together to complete a task and then return to a disaggregated state when the task is completed.

"There is absolutely no inevitability as long as there is a willing-
ness to contemplate what is happening." [9]

—MARSHALL MCLUHAN

An increasing population, changing demographics, and rapid technological change will combine to introduce a tension into future society that may lead to conflict. What will we do to avoid such conflict? First, and most importantly, we will embrace change. Although we will continue to stress the development of science and technology, our ability to survive will really be more about *culture* and how we handle change, our ability to handle change in drastic ways and in short periods of time. We will do this by recognizing that the metric of individual value will be related more to what a person has to contribute, and less to their status, age, level of experience, or background, something the information age has already done. We will leverage diversity through collaboration. We will empower our "Strategic Corporals" (a term given to junior members of a military organization who, because of the advances of the information age, can take actions that have strategic implications) and their civilian counterparts. We will think "out of the box." We will challenge the status quo. We will ask the hard questions and not accept the traditional "schoolbook" solution. We will conduct historical research and trend analysis but will not rely exclusively on these tools. We will examine the second and third order consequences of actions and events, and understand that events do not occur in isolation, but rather are linked and integrated in both cause and effect. We will realize that there is no such thing as "perfect information," or the "perfect decision," and that we'll not be 100 percent accurate 100 percent of the time. We will stress organizational speed and agility over optimization. We will progress from twentieth-century processes to twenty-first-century integrated approaches. The year 2058 looks bright because our people are prepared for the increased responsibility that the information age demands in order to be successful. The "Strategic Corporal" is ready.

15

Jody Williams

*Jody Williams is a human rights activist who was awarded the Nobel
Peace Prize in 1997, along with the International Campaign to Ban
Landmines (ICBL), for her role as the founding coordinator of the ICBL,
which achieved its goal of an international treaty banning antipersonnel
landmines. She is now campaign ambassador of ICBL and founder of
Nobel Women's Initiative, a united effort to help strengthen work being
done in support of women's rights around the world. Forbes Magazine
has named her one of the 100 most powerful women in the world.*

WILL WE BE 50 YEARS FROM TODAY?

That question is perhaps a pessimistic beginning from someone who sincerely
believes—and acts upon the belief—that when committed people take action,
positive change is more than possible. But like so many, I also believe we are
at a serious crossroads and the probable futures we face depend upon the roads
taken every day—individually and collectively.

We are confronted with a dramatically changed global environment, which
is changing even more dramatically with each passing day. Global warming
and environmental devastation; massive migrations and human traffick-
ing; HIV/AIDS and other global health menaces; weapons proliferation
and the brink of a new nuclear arms race; terrorism—by states, networks,

and individuals; widespread violence against women—during war and during "peace." The list is long and quite overwhelming to think about all in one sentence.

But we can be the keepers of our fate, and that of the entire planet, if we are willing to accept these new challenges with new responses for our collective well-being—our collective security. Like it or not, we cannot escape each other and the reality that what happens "there" has an impact "here" and what we do from "here" has an impact "there" and "there" and "there." That being the case, it is time to think about "people-centered" security rather than the traditional state-centric notion that has shaped thinking for centuries—and which I would argue is out of step with meeting the needs of our times.

It is time to think about "people-centered" security rather than the traditional state-centric notion that has shaped thinking for centuries.

Individuals and individual communities generally see threat and security quite differently from how states understand them. For most of the billions living on this planet, the threats they face include finding drinking water at all—let alone clean drinking water. Or how to survive on less than two dollars a day. Or how to decide which child might have the privilege of a few years of education, given that there are not enough resources for everyone to go to school. Or how to protect their children from being stolen and forced to be child soldiers in wars not of their making and that destroy their own families and communities. Or how to protect their children from the massive proliferation of guns and other weapons that threaten them on the city streets where they live and play. Or how to promote human rights and gender equality in states that would see you dead for such activities.

For these billions, the fight between the United States and Russia over anti-missile deployment in former Eastern Bloc nations does not hit their radar screen. For these billions, the struggles over the weaponization of space are beyond their interest. For these billions, it is fair to guess that if they were even aware of the billions of dollars that the United States alone spends on its nuclear weapons programs each year, they would argue that their real security would be better met by spending those billions on health, education, clean water, and basic housing.

What most seek and all deserve are the most basic of freedoms, as noted in the UN Charter—freedom from want and freedom from fear. They seek and deserve a say in their own future, a future worth living for—with hope for themselves and for their children and for their children's children. They are seeking peace that is not defined by the simple absence of armed conflict. Sustainable peace— real peace—that can only rest on global socioeconomic justice and equality in a world where our scarce resources are shared and our environment protected. They may not be able to name it, but they are seeking human security—a concept still not well articulated and even less well acted upon.

Perhaps one of the clearest definitions of human security was formulated under the government of Nelson Mandela. It reads: "In the new South Africa national security is no longer viewed as a predominantly military and police problem. It has broadened to incorporate political, economic, social, and environmental matters. At the heart of this new approach is a paramount concern with the *security of people*. Security is an all-encompassing condition in which *individual citizens* live in freedom, peace, and safety; participate fully in the process of governance; enjoy the protection of fundamental rights; have access to resources and the basic necessities of life; and inhabit an environment which is not detrimental to their health and well-being."

It seems like a daunting and overwhelming task—downright utopian! But I believe that if we are to have hope for a viable future fifty years from today, we must embrace human security, multilateralism, and collective responses to our collective challenges. We are already in many ways trying to deal with the various elements outlined above—reinforcing good governance, trying to reduce extreme poverty, responding to environmental crises, mitigating economic globalization's negative effects. What we must do is weave these threads into an overarching strategy to address the direct and indirect threats that people really face every day of their lives. And even more important, we must devise the means to implement this strategy.

But where would the money come from? Many argue the costs would be impossible to meet. One suggestion would be for the nations of the world to act upon the responsibility they accepted as member states of the United Nations and begin implementing Article 26 of the UN Charter. That article, ignored now for more than fifty years, calls upon the Security Council to formulate plans for a system to regulate weapons "in order to promote the establishment and maintenance of international peace and security with the least diversion for armaments of the world's human and economic resources. . . ." In other words, stop the production and proliferation of the means of war, death, and destruction, and use those resources for the common good.

Already, military spending and the global weapons trade constitute the largest area of spending in the world—over one trillion dollars—and it is growing annually. The United States alone spends more than all other countries combined. In 2006, the government spent 52 percent of our money on defense, while allocating 6.3 percent to health and 5.3 percent to education. By mid-2007, the United States was spending approximately $13 billion a month on the war in Iraq. Why is it possible to "find" billions for war, but virtually nothing to combat the real threats people face?

Imagine even a small adjustment in the percentages spent on war, making and shifting that money to health, education, poverty alleviation, addressing climate change—by not only the United States but all the countries of the world. Imagine a world that puts the security of individuals over the security of the state. Imagine a world described by Nelson Mandela's government, where "[s]ecurity is an all-encompassing condition in which *individual citizens* live in freedom, peace, and safety; participate fully in the process of governance; enjoy the protection of fundamental rights; have access to resources and the basic necessities of life; and inhabit an environment which is not detrimental to their health and well-being."

If we can move beyond imaging it and work together to bring it about, our world could be a very different place fifty years from today. If we continue down our current path, will we even *be* fifty years from today?

16

Kim Dae-jung

Kim Dae-jung is the former president of the Republic of Korea. He was awarded the Nobel Peace Prize in 2000 for his work for democracy and human rights in South Korea and in East Asia in general, and for peace and reconciliation with North Korea in particular.

THE ERA OF GREAT CHANGE IS COMING

Fifty years from today, mankind will encounter the era of the fastest changes in history. Remarkable developments will be witnessed in every field of human society and make great differences to the human life and mother earth.

First, outer space will appear in a new form. Aerospace industries will be embodied, and space stations, as well as space cities, will be established. Mankind will acquire unlimited resources of new energy and minerals through the access to space. In the middle of such progress, the secret behind the formation of the universe will unfold.

Second, the era of the ocean will arrive. The use and development of ocean resources will rapidly grow, and minerals at the deep ocean bottom will be explored in full scale. Also, underwater metropolises will be built. Ships armed with high speed and supersized will bring the revolution of transportation. The marine and fishery industry will recede and be transferred to a new era of aquaculture.

Third, the era of robots and artificial intelligence will be ushered in. As

robots and computers take the place of human intelligence, the social class between the white-collar and the blue-collar workers will disappear. Artificial intelligence systems faster and more convenient than the human brain will uphold such an era. At that time, people will be able to communicate simply by thinking.

Fourth, nationalism will be gone, and globalization will come. Due to the development of a global network system, people will make their living beyond the influence of "state-nation" throughout every field, and a state-nation will rather become a kind of grand social organization. All the cultures on earth will be crossed and combined. Simultaneous translation of all languages will be enabled. The international society, although there is skepticism, is likely to be led by *Chindia* and the *BRICs* (Brazil, Russia, India, and China).

Fifth, the awakening as well as resistance of the poor and strengthened consciousness on human justice will help the problem of polarization between the rich and the poor ease greatly. Environmental pollution will be dramatically reduced, and polluted earth will be able to restore its purity.

Sixth, marvelous progress in medical technology will be accomplished. Improvements in molecular biology will reveal the origin of life and ultimately enable people to live more than one hundred years. Through medications, people will be able to not only cure damaged organs, nerves, and skin, but also to regenerate healthy ones. The use of the substitutive organs produced by cloning will be active, and cerebral nerves will be successfully replaced.

However, there are some negative prospects.

First of all, as the 5 percent of human population dominates 95 percent of the entire human wealth, terror, rebellions, and wars of the underprivileged class may lead mankind to cause dire conditions. Second, there is a possibility of catastrophe upon human beings due to deterioration of environment caused by climate change and water pollution. Third, conflicts between humans and robots as a result of the development of artificial intelligence may occur. Additionally, on account of the extreme informatization, individual privacy may be violated more than it was in the medieval times. When these negative scenarios of the future are thoroughly prepared for and overcome, human beings and mother earth will be able to open the door of the very bright future.

17

Ronald Noble

Ronald Noble is secretary general of Interpol, the world's largest
international police organization.

The Future of Crime

Today, if one watches television, reads newspapers, or surfs the Internet, he or she might conclude that Al Qaeda-linked or Al Qaeda-inspired terrorists have taken over the planet. Fifty years from today, I see a world in which we have taken it back.

That's the optimist in me talking, because fifty years is a long time away, and we can do much between now and then to reduce, if not eliminate, both the actual and perceived threat of this kind of terrorism.

At first, terrorists seemed to menace citizens and businesses from abroad, and the battle cry was, "Be careful, foreign terrorists can hit you anywhere in the world, at any time." This was one of the lessons following the September 11, 2001, terrorist strikes in the United States. As difficult as that was for the world to accept, police felt that this problem could be dealt with by investigating much more thoroughly "the foreigners in our midst."

Then, following the London and Madrid bombings, as well as several disrupted terrorist plots, the world was introduced to a new breed of "self-radicalized" or "home-grown" terrorists who choose to kill their own neighbors

and fellow citizens—in the very communities to which they belonged and that nourished them. The world is now coming to grips with the fact that the Internet's vast reach enables terrorists to spread their deadly propaganda, obtain recruits, provide training, raise funds, and plan their attacks on a global basis. Extremist and violent ideologies are reaching and influencing people of all walks of life—of every age, gender, ethnicity, and socioeconomic status—so we cannot tell where the next suicide bomber will come from, or when, where, or why he or she will next strike.

On top of all this, it is only a matter of time before new waves of terrorists begin spilling out of places like Iraq and Afghanistan—where they are learning their deadly arts and becoming battle hardened.

All of this could cause someone to see the world of tomorrow as a place of doom and gloom. But not me. From my vantage point, I can see the storm on the horizon. Yet I can also see what can be done to weather that storm—to put in place better structures, systems, policies, and practices in order to prevent this storm from causing long-lasting harm to all of us who believe in free and open societies guided by the rule of law.

Weathering this storm cannot occur, however, unless the world's leaders, citizens, and bureaucracies concerned with security recognize that we need to shift from an emphasis on the military to an emphasis on law enforcement. This will allow us to focus more on prevention, rather than on the weapons and strength of the military.

Military action is required to defeat standing armies in specific locations. But terrorists do not employ standing armies, and terror-

Over a fifty-year period, the prevention of terrorism is more properly a police function, rather than a military one.

ists can be found anywhere. Like other criminal networks, they employ ordinary citizens who move among us through ordinary channels right up until the point of their attack (particularly, but by no means exclusively, in cases of home-grown terrorism). This is why, over a fifty-year period, the prevention of terrorism is more properly a police function, rather than a military one.

We need to reinforce our global network of international police cooperation to construct a global network of tripwires that will prevent the free movement of terrorists and will alert police nationally and internationally when terrorists are plotting to carry out their attacks. In this regard, the world's governments and citizens need to think and act more like the private sector rather than the public sector.

Let me use an analogy from the private sector to illustrate the world that I see in fifty years. Think about how the credit card industry works globally. Think of credit card issuers as countries and credit cards as passports. And then consider the global private security network that allows the cards to be used and verified anywhere in the world at any time of day or night. The credit card issuers know when, where, and how their cards are being used by cardholders, and they know when that activity is suspicious or dangerous to the well-being of the issuer.

In fifty years, governments will be able to know when, where, and how their passports are being used. They will know where people are going and what transactions they are engaging in. So they will be able to know whether a person's travel pattern, bank activity, or other transactions are suspicious or dangerous.

But to accomplish this, the world will have to confront many thorny issues. One major issue is privacy. What will the expectations of privacy be for citizens in fifty years? Will they accept governments having as much information stored about them and accessible to the police as they now accept regarding companies with which they do business? Will governments be able to trace the movements of people worldwide through technology and through a network of institutions? Will they be able to analyze such movement in a way that will highlight unusual international travel or activity? Right now, for example, there are governments experimenting with travel pattern monitors that read license plates to determine which cars enter which neighborhoods during which hours, in order to identify anomalies and to match these anomalies with robberies or burglaries. Will this kind of monitoring become the norm for all travel, both domestic and international? I believe the answer to most of these questions will be yes.

Privacy is important, yet it must be balanced against the need for governments to have the information required to effectively prevent terrorist attacks. And as the terrorist threats mount, as I believe they will, the balance will weigh more heavily toward safety and security. I am not talking about a reduction of liberty, or even of privacy in its truest sense (i.e., I am not saying that governments will be peering into our homes), but, rather, I am saying that people will no longer be able to travel and engage in transactions with anonymity. In other words, governments will know where people are going and what they are doing in the public realm. This will be accomplished through extensive use of cameras, biometrics (e.g., retinal scans, fingerprints, and facial recognition software), full body scans, and perhaps even implanted microchips (as we now do with some pets and children), plus scanning of passports at airports and other border entry points, as well as more intensive monitoring of financial and other transactions, and of the Internet (terrorist organizations employ thousands of Web sites, chat rooms, electronic billboards, and e-mails).

People will no longer be able to travel and engage in transactions with anonymity. In other words, governments will know where people are going and what they are doing in the public realm.

The world is already moving in this direction. Indeed, some social commentators have opined that we live in the "post-privacy era." There are already many cameras deployed throughout many major cities, for example. The difference that I see happening is that fifty years from now the surveillance will be much more extensive and the resultant information will be much more completely integrated and analyzed.

Right now, much of the information that is available to the government is incomplete and fragmented. Information from cameras goes to one agency, while information about international travel or financial transactions goes to other agencies, etc. Fifty years from now, I envision a world in which information about people's movements and transactions will be collected and sent to intelligence "fusion" centers, where the information will be analyzed in order to spot indicators of actual or potential terrorist and other criminal activities.

In addition to such changes at the national levels, I believe there will also be major changes at the international level. The campaign against terrorism and other international crime requires a comprehensive global law enforcement model. This means a fundamental paradigm shift from the current approach, which is a patchwork quilt of disparate and disjointed national, bi-lateral, and/or regional systems that are riddled with gaps—gaps through which terrorist and other criminal networks are spreading their tentacles and engulfing the planet. Fifty years from now, I envision a world in which advanced technologies, coupled with new concepts regarding expectations of privacy, will allow countries to almost instantly share information and analysis with one another in a truly coordinated and comprehensive manner.

In terms of achieving such enhanced global law enforcement cooperation, I am encouraged by what I have seen in recent years. I have seen that police throughout Interpol's member countries have been working hard to help us develop an array of powerful international law enforcement tools. But, just as the invention of the Internet represented a paradigm shift that could not be actualized until it was widely adopted, so, too, is it the case regarding the tools of international law enforcement today. Fifty years from today, however, I see a world in which governments had long before recognized the urgent need to actualize the paradigm shift that must occur in global law enforcement—a world in which the tools of international law enforcement have been fully deployed and universally utilized within a comprehensive global system that is properly resourced and supported by the world's governments. We must create such a system. This, I believe, is the challenge of our time. How we, as a world community, respond to this challenge will determine our future.

18

Norman E. Borlaug

Norman E. Borlaug is an agricultural scientist who was awarded the Nobel Peace Prize in 1970 for his contributions to world peace through increasing food supply. Called "the Father of the Green Revolution," he has contributed to the growth of high-yielding wheat varieties, based partly on his research, on 200 million acres in the world. He is the recipient of the US Presidential Medals of Freedom and Science, the US Congressional Gold Medal, and the National Service Medal of the US National Academies of Science.

THE FUTURE OF FOOD

The Past

Over the past fifty years, a world revolution in agriculture has occurred. Thanks to a continuing stream of research and technological advances, the world's farmers and ranchers have been able to increase the world food supply faster than the growth in human population numbers. Between 1950 and 2000, world cereal production rose from 650 million tons in 1950, while global population increased 2.5 times. Per capita food availability has improved, and perhaps two billion people have been rescued from chronic hunger. And for the first time in history, food production was mainly increased by raising grain yields per acre rather than bringing more land under the plow. Indeed, the tripling in world cereal production occurred with only a 10 percent increase in cultivated area. Had we attempted to produce the world cereal harvest of 2000 with the agricultural technology of 1950, we would have to have added three billion acres of new land for cereal production, land that the world no longer had readily available without cutting down forests and plowing up grasslands.

Today, much of the global land area suitable for agricultural production is already in use. In densely populated Asia, in particular, some of the land currently used by farmers should be taken out of production to preserve the environment. Perhaps as much as three-fourths of future increases in food production will have to come from lands already in use. Many of these lands, such as in the industrialized nations, already are being intensively farmed, and already are producing close to their theoretical potential with currently available technology. Thus, future gains in food production will be harder to come by than in the past. This will require significant investments in research—by public and private organizations—if we are to meet the formidable food, fiber, and industrial agriculture demands of the next fifty years, and to do so in environmentally friendly ways.

The Future

The United Nations has predicted that world population will peak at about 9 billion toward the middle of the twenty-first century, and then begin to decline. However, I think this number is overly conservative. Because of the continuing high levels of rural illiteracy and poverty affecting more than half of the world's people, I believe that world population will grow more quickly, and will likely reach ten billion by 2050, before possibly beginning to decline. This is roughly 3.5 billion more people than inhabit the planet Earth today. Almost all of the growth in projected human numbers will occur in the developing countries, with sub-Saharan Africa (even with the HIV/AIDS pandemic) posting the greatest percentage gains, followed by South Asia and the predominantly Muslim countries.

Throughout history, the growth in global food demand has been dictated by two factors: increases in human numbers and increases in human wealth, which shifts diets from ones in which most calories come from consuming plants to ones where most calories come from consuming animal food products. Growth in global wealth in some of the newly industrializing nations clearly shows this shift to greater consumption of animal and fish products which, in turn, depend largely upon cereal grains and oilseeds for their feed.

Global food and feed demand in 2050 is likely to increase by 75 percent over today, and this figure could be much higher, if large quantities of food and feed crops are diverted to making ethanol and other biofuels. This means that, within the next fifty years, global consumers are likely to require an annual world agricultural production that is double the level of today—from 5.5 billion gross metric tons to 11 billion gross tons. This is an enormous task, one that will put enormous environmental pressure on global land and water resources. It will require what some have called a "doubly Green Revolution," where principles of science and technology are applied, not only to food and feed production, but also to environmental preservation.

Global food and feed demand in 2050 is likely to increase by 75 percent over today, and this figure could be much higher, if large quantities of food and feed crops are diverted to making ethanol and other biofuels.

Growing scarcity of water will require that the twenty-first century will need to bring about a "Blue Revolution," one in which water-use productivity is much more closely wedded to land-use productivity. Continued genetic improvement of food crops—using conventional and biotechnology research tools—is needed to shift the yield frontier higher and to increase stability of yield. Irrigated lands will continue to contribute a disproportionate portion of world food supplies.

There has been considerable debate within the scientific community about what to do about global warming. Some, myself included, have argued that it is better to concentrate on adapting to the effects than try to reverse climate change, which may not be possible anyway. Others have said that through collective international cooperation, we can mitigate and even reverse climate change, and do so within reasonable economic costs. As more scientific information becomes available, it is clear that both strategies are urgently needed.

There is no doubt that global warming is occurring, and possibly faster than previously predicted. There is increasing evidence that over the next fifty years agriculture in the tropics and subtropics will be ever-more challenged by increasing drought and higher temperatures. This has serious consequences for the developing world, especially Africa, where the poor will be ill-equipped to deal with the production consequences of these changes. On the other hand, agriculture in temperate zones, such as the USA and Canada, will likely benefit from the warming temperatures.

By the end of 2007, it is likely that one-third of the US corn harvest is going to ethanol production. There is a risk of converting so much grain into fuel for cars that it will drive up the price of grain in world grain markets. Over the longer term, there are better raw materials for ethanol production than food crops. Cellulosic ethanol, made from trees and fibrous plants—and wastes from the wood and paper products industry—is eventually where we want to be, since this raw material will not compete with food crop demand. But we still lack a cost-effective way to break down cellulous fiber for conversion into ethanol.

Biotechnology based upon recombinant DNA has developed invaluable new scientific methodologies and products in food and agriculture. This journey deeper into the genome—to the molecular level—is the continuation of our progressive understanding of the workings of nature. Recombinant DNA methods have enabled breeders to select and transfer single genes, which has not only reduced the time needed in conventional breeding to eliminate undesirable genes, but also allowed breeders to access useful genes from other distant species.

Current genetically modified crop varieties that help to control insects and weeds are lowering production costs and increasing harvests. In preparing agriculture to adapt to changing climate, the new tools of biotechnology will be invaluable to develop crop varieties with greater tolerance of drought, waterlogging, heat, and cold. Future genetically modified products are likely to carry traits that will improve nutrition and health.

The needless confrontation of consumers against the use of transgenic crop technology in Europe and elsewhere might have been avoided had more people received a better education in biological science. Privileged societies have the luxury of adopting a very low-risk position on the genetically modified crops issue, even if this action later turns out to be unnecessary. But the vast majority of humankind does not have such a luxury, and certainly not the hungry victims of wars, natural disasters, and economic crises.

We cannot turn back the clock and use the agricultural technology of an earlier day. This includes shifting from high-yield agriculture to so-called organic production technology, where no chemical fertilizers or crop protection chemicals are used. Wealthy consumers can afford the luxury of organic fruits, vegetables, and meat, but the poor cannot. I have seen reliable estimates that organic forms of agriculture can probably only support a world of four billion people.

The world has the technical capacity and financial resources to assure food security for ten billion people. The more pertinent question is whether it has the political and ethical will to do so.

Lest we forget, peace will not be built upon empty stomachs or human misery.

19

Richard Clarke

*Richard Clarke served as national coordinator for security and
counterterrorism for President Clinton and President George W. Bush.
He was the special adviser to the president for Cyberspace Security and
chairman of the president's Critical Infrastructure Protection Board. He
is chairman of Good Harbor Consulting and the author of* Against All
Enemies *and* Scorpion's Gate, *a novel of espionage and counterterrorism set in a not-too-distant future.*

WHAT DOES IT MEAN TO BE HUMAN?

Several decades hence, the burning political, economic, and social issues of
the day will not be terrorism and war, or abortion and stem cell research. The
issue may be something far more profound: what does it mean to be human?

At a technical level, setting aside concepts of souls and divinities, that question can be easily answered in 2008. We humans are a carbon-based life form,
biologically produced by human reproduction, with a biochemical brain
capable of more advanced processing than any other life form we know. What
will happen to make that change?

Science and technological advances are building upon each other, greatly
accelerating the pace of change. The convergence of progress in biotechnology,
computer science, nanotechnology, artificial intelligence, human-machine

interfaces, and the study of the human brain will bring about revolutionary change over the next three decades. The transformation that results will change the way we live far more profoundly than the Industrial Revolution or the recent information technology revolution. And it will create political issues that will dominate society.

I stumbled upon the building blocks of the coming changes when researching my second novel, *Breakpoint*. In that thriller I tried to portray a world on the edge of realizing what was about to happen, a world already feeling the political impact of massive and sweeping technologically driven change. All of the technologies that I envisioned in *Breakpoint* exist today in laboratories and research programs.

For example, the debate today about base-ball players using steroids and other pharmaceuticals to enhance their performance is just the beginning of the debate about human enhancement. While today we think of artificial hips and knees as normal, defense research is now providing amputees with limbs that out-perform their original arms and legs. The Pentagon is also beginning to create exoskeleton suits. Soldiers will be able to climb inside bullet-resistant suits that would monitor their body functions. When their heart rates increase, or they overheat, or their blood sugar drops, or they are injured, the suit (perhaps in consultation with a remote doctor or computer) will administer the needed drugs or other first aid. The suit will literally give the solider eyes in the back of her head, projecting images on the viewscreen in her helmet. Images from miniature robotic devices in the air or around the corner will extend the soldier's situational awareness. Infra red and telescopic optics will give the soldier Superman's vision. Some of Superman's strength will come from servo-motors in the suit's arms and legs, giving the soldier the ability to lift objects weighing many times her body weight, or to run at Olympic athletes' speeds.

> *Soldiers will be able to climb inside bullet-resistant suits that would monitor their body functions.*

Human-machine interfaces (HMIs) are happening already. People with diminished hearing can now buy hearing aids that are also linked to their mobile telephones, so that what allows them to hear things happening nearby will also connect them to Internet packets carrying voice through cyberspace. Some born completely deaf have already benefited from artificial cochlear devices tied to nerves running directly to the brain. Paralyzed patients are today using brain waves to move computer mice and keyboards. Powered HMI implants in the body, connected directly to the brain, are showing promise in dealing with some forms of depression and epilepsy. Work is underway on artificial retinas for the blind, which will also involve direct connections to the brain. Researchers are attempting to reverse engineer the human brain by constructing a computer with the same design.

That is all occurring today. Several decades out, it is entirely possible that we will be able to have our biological brains, with their memories formed by hormones and other chemicals, interacting directly with silicon-based computer memory chips and related devices. This raises the prospect of adding memory to human brains, just as we do today to our old laptops. If we can do that, we can also download human brain memory into remote storage devices. That memory could outlive the human life form that created it. The human brain, connected directly to devices that can tie to cyberspace, could expand its available memory by accessing all human knowledge stored on networks throughout the world.

The ultimate HMIs would be nanodevices, highly capable machines so small they are almost invisible to the normal human eye. The US government is investing billions of dollars in nanoresearch. One application could eventually be nanomachines that move through the human body detecting and perhaps correcting cancers and other disorders. Beyond machines in the body, drugs will also add capability and lengthen life.

The Performance Enhancing Pharmaceuticals (PEPs) that allow athletes to hit more home runs may be controversial, but who will object to pharmacological advances that prevent brain degradation by Alzheimer's disease? Similar PEPs may be able to enhance memory. What if you could take a pill while studying for a final exam and the information studied would be placed into long-term memory? Defense Department research is developing drugs that will allow soldiers to go for days without sleep, perhaps with heightened awareness and with no negative side effects. Other drugs may be able to stop or dramatically slow aging by altering telomeres at the tips of our chromosomes. Aging may also be addressed by stem cell utilization. Already researchers have grown a human bladder. Decades from now, replacing organs grown from our own stem cells may also be routine.

Genetic engineering offers the prospect for eliminating inherited defects like sickle-cell anemia. The same techniques, however, could enhance human capability by making rare mental and physical capabilities routine.

Decades from now, replacing organs grown from our own stem cells may also be routine.

While the human body is being enhanced by drugs, devices, and HMIs, machines themselves will also be growing in capability. Today robots assemble automobiles and look for bombs. In the near term, robots will tend to human patients, providing the aging with companionship, giving them their pills on time, and calling emergency services when the human falls or is taken ill. Many more tasks now performed by humans will be performed by robotic devices in the next several decades.

Computers have talked directly to other computers for years. Artificial Intelligence (AI) software programs today make decisions that run computer, telephone, electric power, financial, and other networks. AI is beginning to perform medical diagnoses better than human doctors. AI software may be used to write other software, reducing the many errors now routinely made by human programmers. The world's largest supercomputers in Europe, Asia, and America are now being directly linked. New computers using quantum techniques and photonics will be deployed in the next decades, massively increasing computational capability.

How will all of that technology change society? For those with full access to the technology, life could be significantly prolonged through stem cell-grown organ replacements, pharmaceutically slowed aging, and genetic engineering that removes health threats. Human capability could be enormously enhanced through genetic alteration, implants, nanotech devices, human machine interfaces, artificial body parts, and direct connections to smart robots and networks of computers accessing all human knowledge. Compared to people in the nineteenth century, some in 2060 will be superhumans. Others will not be. For the first time, the rich might actually be more intelligent. Life extension could accelerate overpopulation or alter the traditional multigenerational family structure.

Just as today there are marked differences in life expectancy and quality of life for people living in various locations around the globe, those without access to the new technologies could be objectively less intelligent, physically weaker, shorter-lived. The implications for democracy could be profound. Nations used to engaging in arms races could be competing instead in developing and deploying human enhancements, HMIs, and robotics.

People will have so many computers in their bodies and such connectivity to networks with AI systems that there will be questions about where the line is between humans and machines.

Issues of bioethics will make the current stem cell, abortion, and evolution debates look mild. Which PEPs should be permitted and which made illegal, forced into the drug underworld as cocaine and heroine are today? Should we go beyond fixing defects to enhancing human capability? Who should get which enhancements and who should pay for them? Are we, by changing the human genome, beginning to play God? Humans could, in effect, take control of their own biological evolution, the first species ever to do so. We will be debating whether the ultimate path of evolution always was for a species to emerge that would have sufficient self-knowledge to fix its defects and design new capabilities. Some claim that the enhanced are not humans.

Simultaneously, society will debate the expanding roles and capabilities of machines, robots, and other computers. People will have so many computers in their bodies and such connectivity to networks with AI systems that there will be questions about where the line is between humans and machines. The genetically enhanced humans and the devices inside them will be networked into massive global grid information systems. Advanced AI will resemble life forms in important respects. Will humans, originally carbon-based life forms, live peacefully with or blend with computers, silicon-based life forms? *What does it mean to be human?* will be a real question. For the first time, the answer may be different in fifty years.

There will be those who will seek to place a cap on scientific progress in these areas, based on religious arguments. Others will seek to slow down the pace of progress to minimize the risk of disastrous mistakes.

The people who will make these decisions are not in some science fiction fantasy. Some of these decisions are already being made by people who are alive right now. Will the post-enhancement human race look back on us as a lower life form, the way we see the Neanderthal or maybe even the way we see the life forms that first emerged onto land? Perhaps, unless, of course, we first so damage the world by climate change or nuclear or biological war that our global society retreats technologically, as it did in the Dark Ages. It is not presumptuous to think that the next fifty years may be the most important in the history of life on Earth.

20

Richard Restak

Richard Restak is a neurologist and neuropsychiatrist and the author of eighteen books on the human brain, including The Naked Brain: How the Emerging Neurosociety Is Changing·How We Live, Work, and Love. *He is president of the American Neuropsychiatric Association.*

A BRAIN SCIENTIST'S PERSPECTIVE

By 2058, new technological developments will be the driving force leading to brain science-inspired behavioral and lifestyle changes. For instance, inexpensive, easily employed instruments will enable monitoring and identification of internal mental states. As a benefit, people will no longer be under the sway of uncontrollable mood swings or remain "out of touch" with their feelings. Thanks to these instruments, personality traits like extroversion, altruism, love, patriotism, empathy, risk taking, and violence will be understood for the first time in terms of chemical, electrical, and magnetic activity patterns within the brain. These breakthroughs will spur national debates about whether it is permissible to use this technology to stimulate healthy mental states in as many people as possible in the interest of creating a more harmonious society.

Emotional and behavioral disorders will be treated with specially designed drugs synthesized on the basis of a combination of cellular DNA analysis and the manipulation of the tissue concentrations of between twenty-five and thirty biochemical compounds in different brain areas. Just prior to starting the drug, a scan will be carried out providing a color-coded printout that serves as the equivalent of a brain "fingerprint" that identifies the unique patterns of neurotransmitter-receptor interaction, blood flow, electric activity, and metabolism in each patient's brain.

Drugs will be aimed not only at helping the patient feel better but also at correcting the unique gene and neurotransmitter malfunctions responsible for each disease. And because the drugs will be especially designed for each patient, side effects won't occur. Nor will the drugs exert any other action in the patient's body. For the first time in history, cures rather than just symptom relief will be possible for neurological and psychiatric illnesses.

> *For the first time in history, cures rather than just symptom relief will be possible for neurological and psychiatric illnesses.*

Nor will all of the advances in the application of brain science to the world of 2058 be limited to biology. Neuroprosthetics (the interface of brains and machines) will make it possible to compensate for losses of vision and hearing. This breakthrough will be the culmination of experimental research dating from the early years of the twenty-first century, which showed that if nerve impulses from an animal's eye are shunted to the auditory rather than the visual cortex of the animal's brain, the auditory cells are able to process vision in addition to sound. In fifty years, this process will be sufficiently perfected so that it can be applied to humans.

A child who is born blind will have signals from the eye wirelessly rerouted to the auditory cortex, which will then process both sight and hearing. A child who is born deaf will undergo a similar routing of impulses from the ear to the visual cortex, which will then process hearing as well as vision. And since there will be no need for surgery, both of these procedures can be easily and safely applied to blind and deaf babies. Thus blindness and deafness will be essentially eradicated in countries with the means and facilities to take advantage of this technology.

Accompanying these developments will be the evolution of the "neuron tran-sistor"—a fusion of the "wet" form of biological information processing using living tissues with digital electronics. Nanorobots (also known as nanobots) incorporated into the brain will provide feedback about activities in selected brain areas. These tiny structures, only a small fraction of the size of a living cell and visible only to the most powerful microscopes, will provide second-by-second monitoring of the brain. A third generation version of the nanoantenna, first patented in 2007, will receive signals that will abort seizures, inhibit tremors, and repair brain cells damaged by stroke or traumatic brain injury.

Another application of nanotechnology will enable paralyzed people to regain their ability to walk, thanks to the injection of molecules into the spinal cord that self-assemble into nanofibers—thousands of times thinner than a human hair—that prevent the formation of harmful scar tissue and promote the regeneration of lost or damaged cells.

Other developments that we can expect by 2058 include:

- Remaining "connected" will no longer require cell phones or comput-ers. Microprocessors will be sufficiently miniaturized so that they can be wirelessly connected with the brain and act as "intelligence assis-tants" for routing information outside the usual sensory channels of sight, hearing, touch, etc.

- Imaging devices will be available capable of monitoring the brains of several people at the same time. This new technology will provide a window on the mechanisms of social interaction by demonstrating how one person's brain activity influences the brains of others. Brain signatures for empathy will identify people who share common assumptions and similar emotional responses. Such insights will allow for new kinds of focus groups based on the responses of many people as they simultaneously undergo experiences such as listening to a political speech or attending a presidential debate.

- Thanks to memory-enhancing drugs, superpower memories will become commonplace. But this may well turn out to be a mixed blessing since mental health often requires forgetting rather than remembering, particularly in response to traumatic experiences. Forgetfulness in such instances will be aided by over-the-counter drugs capable of eliminating established painful memories and inhibiting the formation of new ones.

- Brain science will make major contributions to our understanding of long-debated social and ethical questions ranging from the profound ("Why is war endemic to every civilization in history irrespective of the wealth or education of its citizens?") to the comparatively trivial ("How does one devise a targeted marketing campaign that takes full advantage of customers' brain responses to specific advertisements?").

But the greatest innovation will take place in our educational system. By 2058, the applications of brain science to everyday life will be so extensive and influential that, starting in the primary grades, instruction about the brain will become a regular part of the school curriculum. And although not everyone will be a "brain specialist," some knowledge about the brain will be considered indispensable for personal and occupational success in the later part of the twenty-first century.

21

Sandra Postel

Sandra Postel is director of the Global Water Policy Project and current director of the Center for the Environment at Mount Holyoke College. She is the author of Last Oasis: Facing Water Scarcity, *the basis of a PBS documentary,* Pillar of Sand: Can the Irrigation Miracle Last?, *and co-author of* Rivers for Life: Managing Water for People and Nature. *Postel is a 1995 Pew Scholar in Conservation and the Environment and, in 2002, was named one of the "Scientific American 50" by* Scientific American *magazine, an award recognizing contributions to science and technology.*

IN HARMONY WITH EARTH'S WATER CYCLE

A little over a decade ago, I stood on desiccated Earth in the degraded delta of the Colorado River and listened to an elder Cocopa Indian, whose people had fished and farmed in the delta for more than a thousand years, say, "I hope one day to see the river rise again."

The Colorado was one of the first major rivers to be dammed, diverted, and depleted into oblivion before reaching the sea. It happened to the Colorado in the early 1960s, but since then the Yellow River of China, the Amu and Syr Darya of Central Asia, the Nile of northeast Africa, the Indus and Ganges of southern Asia, and the Rio Grande of the American Southwest have joined the list of rivers, the blue arteries of the earth, drained dry before their final des-tinations—ecological disconnections as consequential as diverting the blood-stream from its appointed path in the human body.

So for me to join the Cocopa elder in hope for the future is not easy. As I look at the world through a water lens, the trends are not good. To believe we can harmonize human activities with Earth's sustaining water cycles is to believe that a deep transformation in human consciousness and collective action is possible. But that is exactly what I believe.

As I write, the natural world around us is changing far faster than anyone, including scientists, would have imagined even five years ago. Glaciers are melting, seas are rising, rivers and lakes are drying up, lands from Australia to Alabama lie parched from drought, and the prospect of the next Katrina resides just over the horizon. Amid the battery of studies and predictions about the coming impacts of a warming climate, it seems we have already crossed a thresh-old of change that has catapulted us into a new world, one like nothing human-ity has witnessed before.

Until now, we have been like the frog that chooses to stay in the pot of water as the heat is gradually turned up, unable to grasp the dire consequences of incremental change. But now, the shock and surprise at the pace of change in our environment is shaking us out of our stupor. It's time to jump out, for safety's sake, to a different place. By the day, more citizens, corporate leaders, and government officials appear ready to make the leap.

So I believe that fifty years from now our lives in relation to water—the basis of life on the planet—will look very different than it does today. Good health, sufficient food, secure homes, stable livelihoods, recreational enjoyment, spiri-tual inspiration, peace with neighbors—so often these things boil down to water. Is there enough for all? Is it clean? Is it shared fairly? Is it used wisely? Right now, the answer in most of the world is no. But the trends of today only determine the future if they remain unaltered.

When I fast-forward fifty years, I see a redesigned world of water. In it, diseases due to polluted ponds, rivers, and aquifers, which now claim more than two mil-lions lives each year, most of them children under the age of five, are virtually nonexistent, because all people will have access to a safe supply for drinking, bathing, and cooking. Women in poorer countries will have expanded opportunity, because as girls, they attended school instead of spending their days fetching water for their families. They will also choose to have fewer children, confident that those they have will survive.

More rivers will be rivers again. Engineers will have removed or set back flow-confining levees so that floodwaters can spill naturally onto floodplains, rejuvenating fisheries and replenishing groundwater. Cities and towns will have relocated away from flood-prone areas because of the higher risks of costly flood damages as rivers swell with spring runoff from fast-melting mountain snowpacks. Dams and reservoirs providing valuable water and power will be operated so as to also give rivers the volume and timing of flows they need to sustain fish and overall ecological health. Meanwhile, thousands of dams will have been removed, as their ecological downsides and safety risks outweigh their benefits. Sadly, however, the variety of life within rivers will be less diverse, because dams, diversions, pollution, and warmer temperatures will have driven one in three freshwater species to extinction.

> *By irrigating more efficiently and planting crops suited to their local climates, farmers overall will use half as much water for the same amount of crop production as today.*

Our production and consumption of food will look very different from today. Modernized irrigation systems will enable farmers to water their crops more precisely, and new information technologies will enable them to incorporate real-time data on rainfall, evapotranspiration, and other factors into their management decisions. By irrigating more efficiently and planting crops suited to their local climates, farmers overall will use half as much water for the same amount of crop production as today. Organic foods will dominate the marketplace because of their health and environmental benefits. Consumers will also buy more of their food from local farms because of the high cost of transporting food great distances. In cities, people will get most of their vegetables from rooftop gardens. And diets everywhere will include less meat, because the cost and availability of the land and water needed to produce it will have pushed its price considerably upward.

Computers, clothes, cars, and other goods will be made in factories that recycle and reuse all of their water and discharge no pollutants to the environment. The water productivity of national economies—the volume of water used per dollar of GNP—will be up to ten times higher than it is today.

Overall, water management will be less about pipes, pumps, and pouring concrete, and more about ideas, innovation, and ingenuity. The politics of water will have evolved from competition to cooperation, as nations and states realize they have more to gain by sharing the benefits of a healthy, smartly managed watershed than by fighting for the last drop. And cadres of ecological engineers will enable communities to rely on nature's infrastructure—wetlands, floodplains, and forested watersheds—to supply clean water while at the same time preserving habitats for fish and wildlife and natural areas for people to enjoy.

What I have sketched here is not a prediction, but a vision. By envisioning a desired future, we can work with intention to create it.

We live, today, in the decisive decade. Our action—or inaction—during these next few years will determine whether a better world can emerge from the catastrophic change we have unleashed.

22

Gerardus 't Hooft

Gerardus 't Hooft, professor of theoretical physics at Utrecht University in the Netherlands, shared the Nobel Prize in Physics in 1999 for having placed particle physics theory on a firmer mathematical foundation.

How Will Science Transform Human Society?

The question that was asked to me was simple enough: You know what the world looked like in the 1950s, you can see what it looks like today. New scientific developments have had a major impact on our society. Do these transformations continue to take place? Will they happen again? What could we reasonably expect the world to look like in 2050?

Yet speculations on the impact of today's scientific developments on tomorrow's human society are notoriously difficult, and it is instructive to learn from mistakes made in the past. For scientists like me who like to dream about the future, it is sometimes difficult to accept the simple fact that science cannot solve all problems, and often leads to new ones, but this certainly is the case today, and in all reasonableness one may expect the Brave New World of the mid-twenty-first century to have its own troubles. Some developments have taken place at a much slower pace than what people expected in 1950: there has been no explosive increase in manned space travel, we are not surrounded by semi-intelligent robots, and we have not found the cures for many of our diseases, in spite of some fairly spectacular successes. Some technological developments even seem nearly to have come to a halt: bicycles today look nearly identical to the ones of 1950, and our automobiles still work on exactly the same principles; there were only small changes in their appearance. So, also fifty years from now, the world might look much more like the one we live in today than some "futurologists" might want us to believe.

It is the unexpected developments that indeed have had the greatest impact: science in several fields made giant leaps in the decade 1970–1980. While numerous secrets were unveiled that enormously improved our view of the cosmos as well as the subatomic world, the semiconductor industry discovered how to make microscopic devices that can process information at unprecedented speeds and quantities. The personal computer became available to the public at large, and the portable telephone revolutionized even further our abilities to communicate. The Internet has revolutionized the way we pass on information and the way we do commerce. The world has become a lot smaller, and consequently, an unprecedented mix of cultures is taking place. This gives rise to clashes and disputes but also to a vast increase of mutual understanding. Indeed, the question is well posed: What can we expect next?

The easiest thing we scientists can do is point to scientific advances that have not yet been fully exploited. One of those is the availability of information. Detectors of all sorts can be made small, cheap, and in great quantities. The software used in our computers today can still be improved tremendously. We will be flooded by much more information than we actually need. Our GPS systems, as well as many more similar devices, will become indispensable utensils. Although truly intelligent robots will probably not yet exist in 2050, we will be able to find instant answers to practically all of our questions via the Internet. It is quite likely that Information Technology will continue to transform our world into something that we can hardly imagine even today.

Science itself will profit most from this development. Today, the human genome is known. In 2050, probably, the genomes of most living species will be available on the Internet, taking away some of our present concerns about extinction; extinct species can be recreated if needed. Biologists will be fully occupied by the question of how these DNA codes exactly function, and their findings, whatever they are, will have great impact on the medical sciences, as well as on the food industry.

While the world is shrinking further, its total population will continue to increase, although global availability of effective birth control will bring this to a halt, eventually. From purely technological and economical points of view, there is absolutely no need for widespread poverty anywhere in the world, if military conflicts in the more unfortunate areas could be further suppressed. This was already true in 2000, but unfortunately, these situations lead to spiral movements that depend very much on a factor impossible to predict: human behavior. It is questionable whether our response to the ubiquitous availability of highly advanced technology will be as rational as it should be.

Our energy supplies in 2050 will still depend on the availability of crude oil, while renewable energy sources continue to gain a larger share. This means that our problems with the changing climate will be far from over. I suspect there will be serious disputes about the possibilities for large-scale manmade constructions with which we could attempt to influence the climate on this planet, but even though our world seems to be shrinking, this planet will still be too big for that.

Most predictions about manned space travel made in the 1950s turned out to be way over target. My predictions for 2050 will probably also be too optimistic. Perhaps the plans for a manned trip to Mars will be realized, but, if so, such a trip will be a waste of energy and resources. Like the manned excursions to the moon in 1969, the first trip to Mars will be too costly and dangerous to be followed by more regular and lasting manned expeditions. On the contrary, now the moon is within range for a more permanent human presence and even colonization. I think that around 2050 a permanent lunar base may well exist, and having it expand and become self-supporting will be within the technological possibilities, although complete independence from terrestrial resources will not be realized for many more decades. I think that the historical significance of the lunar base will be so evident that it will gain generous support from the public, and further lasting support from the earth will probably continue, but the success of these lunar habitats will strongly depend on how people will react upon setbacks, which may be technical, financial, or political.

Note that big changes might also take place in the world of amusement. Computer games and virtual reality may improve so much in quality that people may find most of their distractions there, rather than in real travel, reading, or attending concerts, theatre, or other performances. And will people still do science in 2050? Of course, there will always be some who do not wish to run along with the crowds but investigate the real world that we live in. Some of my colleagues suspect that most questions concerning the most basic laws of nature will be solved by that time, but, of course, this is extremely unlikely. Rather, we should fear the opposite: progress toward finding the solutions to our problems may well slow down. Particle accelerator facilities may well be able to reach hundreds of TeV (teraelectron volt) per particle, but this will not suffice to get the complete picture of what elementary particles are made of and how they interact. There will still be a future in 2050.

Computer games and virtual reality may improve so much in quality that people may find most of their distractions there, rather than in real travel, reading, or attending concerts, theatre, or other performances.

23

Shigeo Hirose

*Shigeo Hirose is a multi-award-winning professor in the Department of
Mechanical and Aerospace Engineering at the Tokyo Institute of
Technology. He specializes in the creative design of robotic systems.*

WHERE ARE ALL THE ROBOTS?

What kind of life will people have with robots in fifty years? One typical view
depicted in science fiction novels and movies is a society in which people are living together with humanoids, or human-figured, versatile robots. Humanoids
are shown walking around in the street to shop and cleaning the house with a
vacuum cleaner. A humanoid cares for children while the mother is busy with
work in the office. Senior citizens will be taken care of by the humanoids, and
in the golf course, a humanoid teaches beginners how to swing.

Since the shocking debut of Honda's humanoid P2 in 1996, humanoids
have become very popular in Japan, and with mass media having stirred up
their potential, many people now believe that life surrounded by humanoids
is just around the corner. Even the Japanese government believed in this
dream and spent 4.6 billion yen on the Humanoid Robot Project from 1998
to 2003. But is this the real image of our future society? I disagree.

There are four reasons why I cannot share such a view of a future society
with humanoids:

One is the difficulty of realizing the humanoid itself. While Honda's success in stable biped walking and running with P2 and ASIMO is fantastic, this success is not directly connected to the realization of humanoids. Humanoids with versatile functions should have dexterous arms, a body with distributed tactile sensors, a highly intelligent vision system, a lightweight power source, and above all, real artificial intelligence. A robot can be a humanoid only when all of these features are installed into one body. Since starting my study of robotics in 1971, I have observed the development of the field for over thirty-six years. While the development of the CPU has been astounding during this time, artificial intelligence has not seen such advancement, and the development of mechanical and electrical components for robots has been steady but slow. When I extrapolate this fact to the future, I cannot predict that the humanoid will be realized within fifty years from now.

The second reason is based on the consideration of the "natural dissemination of new technology." A lot of new technology will be developed going forward, and researchers will try to use it for the humanoids. But what we should not forget is that such technology is not for humanoids alone. As soon as it is commercialized, it will be applied to all existing machines to make them more advanced and intelligent. Although realization of an all-in-one functional humanoid is extremely difficult, technological improvement of simple, functional machines can be done much more easily and effectively. Therefore, most of the machines will have evolved into robots even though the humanoid won't be complete yet.

Even today, the automobile has hundreds of actuators and is controlled by advanced computer systems, and it can even guide the driver with a GPS navigator. Autonomous vacuum cleaners can move around and clean a room.

If all machines will have evolved into robots, why should people buy a versatile but expensive humanoid in the future? In the future even the humanoid may find it difficult to work because he cannot find old-fashioned vacuum cleaners; instead, he will be surprised to see that a smart robot cleaner finished the task before he could even begin.

The third reason is based on the consideration of the "freedom of design."

The human figure is by no means optimal. When nature designed us, the quadruped animal was *remodeled*. Two front legs had to be used as arms, and the biped was the only selection. However, robot designers have no such restrictions. They have the privilege to select the best shape to fulfill the required tasks. If they are asked to imitate the human figure, too, the robot performance will be greatly reduced.

Humanoid supporters sometimes claim that the human figure is best because this society is made for humans, and our living space is geometrically suited to the human figure. But is it true? There are many counterexamples. The engineers who made a modern sushi bar obviously paid no attention to a humanoid sushi craft; instead, they changed the layout of the shop itself and introduced a revolving conveyer belt.

Robot technology should not be used to interfere with natural human relations and deprive people of their pride and jobs, but should instead be the silent force behind the scenes to support the life of people.

The fourth reason is based on the consideration of the "nature of human beings." Human beings are social creatures. People feel natural and relaxed when they are living with other people. Human beings have maintained this aspect of living for more than one hundred thousand years, since evolving from monkeys, which had to live in groups to protect themselves. This feature of human beings would not change in a short time. When we think about this, we can see the unnaturalness of the view of a future society with humanoids.

Instead of providing humanoids to children, robot technology should be used for the improvement of the office where the mother is working to allow her to take care of the children herself. Senior citizens should be taken care of by young people by providing them with intelligent tools or machines for elderly care. The job of the tutor for a beginning golfer should be reserved for young people who want to earn a living with their beloved physical activities. We should not forget that even after fifty years, there will still be a lot of people who want to have a sense of dignity and satisfaction in doing their jobs. Robot technology should not be used to interfere with natural human relations and deprive people of their pride and jobs, but should instead be the silent force behind the scenes to support the life of people.

If you were to visit the future society, you may find yourself asking, "Where are all the robots?" Actually, you might not find any humanoids in the streets and in houses. People are enjoying family and city life with other people, not with humanoids. But if you observe more closely you may find a lot of robots with diversified shapes at work. The global environment is maintained in the desert and on mountains, the ocean is cleaned by robots, and urban infrastructure such as high-voltage electric power lines, gas, water, and sewage are maintained by robots. Therefore, the answer to the question "Where are all the robots?" would be, "Robots are everywhere, but not in the form of humanoids."

24

Peter Doherty

*Peter Doherty is an immunologist who shared the Nobel Prize in
Medicine in 1996 for discoveries concerning the specificity of the cell-
mediated immune defense. He studies viral immunity and splits his life
between St. Jude Children's Research Hospital, the University of
Melbourne, and the beaches of southeastern Australia. His recent books
include* The Beginner's Guide to Winning the Nobel Prize *and* A Light
History of Hot Air.

WIND FARMING IN POLLYANNA LAND

Anderson Craig hit the start-button on a balmy, 88° F September day. The
SUV unhooked from the household power, then the twin electric motors cut
in and moved it quietly down the dirt drive. The silence disturbed some
people when the HydroElectrics first took over the truck market, so they'd
bought the audio option that simulated the sound of a V8 gas-burner. Now
the only time you'd hear anything like that was when the amplified "potato-
potato-potato" of a Harley ElectroHog drifted through an open window.

Most bikers had never experienced the throbbing power of the real thing,
unless they'd visited Houston's National Oil Museum. Back in 2025, the
Directors had built the Gas Dome where oil-fired engines were still run at
full power under carefully controlled conditions that dealt with greenhouse

emissions. The Harley sound was a great favorite, along with the roar of the Rolls Royce Merlin aero-engine that had powered the Spitfires and Mustangs of more than a century ago. By 2030, of course, most of the remaining oil was being used to make plastics, and it seemed extraordinary that we'd just burned something so valuable.

It was a long haul to Vegas and, though the sun was shining and the carefully cleaned solar panels on the Craigs' big Chevy Suburban would add charge to the high-test Beijing batteries, they'd also have to burn some hydrogen before reaching the luxurious King Edward Plaza. Their clothes pods and the water-tubes that went everywhere with them had been packed the evening before. Fresh ground water was liquid gold and priced accordingly, so why pay to avoid the flat taste of DeSal when he and Jenny had their own spring back in the foothills?

This could be his last International Wind Farmers Conference, and as one of the dwindling number of founding members who was still on the ball, Anderson was up for the opening Keynote for 2058. He had plenty of time to think about what he would say. Marigold and Harrison had already taken over the business, and he no longer needed to worry about the sixty big mills on the property. He'd installed, then cared for those whirling power plants all his adult life and had done such a good job that even the five antique Danish monsters were still pushing out a good amperage. Now his daughter and son-in-law would carry on.

Soon, he and Jenny would be retiring to Santa Barbara, where Hamish was a leading light in the university's Department of Religious Reconciliation. Ham had recently returned from a sabbatical at the Institute for Abrahamic Studies in Qatar, the place that had done so much to educate religious teachers and calm the tensions between the three great faiths of Middle East origin. Andy and Jenny had taken the opportunity to holiday with Ham, Angie, and the grandchildren on those beautiful, serene Lebanese beaches. The counterpoint between the sound of the waves, the church bells, and the chant of the Muezzin calling the faithful to prayer was firmly embedded in his memory.

For a farmer descended from generations of cattle ranchers, Anderson was an eloquent and compelling speaker. A deeply devout man, he'd played a big part in influencing his congregation, then the national church, to embrace the view that the careful stewardship of this good, green world is a primary responsibility for people of faith. Even so, the advocacy of those who shared his conviction would not have carried the day without the cumulating awareness that there was less water to drink, temperatures were inexorably rising, and weather patterns were becoming increasingly unpredictable. That major shift in priorities on the part of the fundamentalist "base," together with the disaffection caused by the disastrous Iraq war, had pretty much destroyed the Old Republican Party and led to a too long (at least for Andy) Democratic ascendance on the national political scene.

The Craigs had always been Republicans, and Andy had also been very influential in pushing the revolutionary changes that returned the party of Dwight Eisenhower, Teddy Roosevelt, and Abe Lincoln to its roots. When the New Republicans finally took back the House in 2020, the GOP was a very different creature. Influenced greatly by their chief strategist, the aging former "Governator," Arnie Schwarzenegger, they'd pushed through the final legislation that mandated a 90 percent reduction in carbon emissions by 2070.

Even more remarkable was the 2023 signing of the international convention that stated: "The deliberate suppression of the science relating to climate change and technology that will alleviate the severity of global warming is a crime against humanity." Of course, the American Congress would never have gone along with that if it hadn't been for the establishment of the International Court of the Americas on US soil and the option of a Presidential Pardon. The crowds of lawyers, journalists, and observers who flocked to the old courthouse in Oxford, Mississippi, when such increasingly rare cases were being tried added a very different character to the town of William Faulkner.

Anderson had thought very carefully about his upcoming convention speech. What his words would reflect was a sense of immense pride in the contribution that the Craigs and their fellow wind farmers had made to cleaning and greening the country he loved so much. Of course, the efforts of the "windies" had been just a part of that extraordinary American energy and determination that had led to the complete reversal of the carbon emissions problem. As the decades passed, they'd watched completely new industries emerge, along with a healthier and in every way happier society as people had gathered into closer communities and rediscovered the delights of a more modest lifestyle while walking and biking about their daily business. The type 2 diabetes epidemic of the first two decades of the twenty-first century had been consigned to history. Apart from the increased exercise, the redirection of the corn syrup industry to biofuel production had also helped.

With America leading, and the institution of tariffs against goods manufactured in countries that would not comply with internationally agreed carbon targets, the rest of the world had quickly followed suit. Remitting carbon taxes back to supply the necessary resources to the poor nations of the planet had also led to a new sense of international accord, and to a view that humanity had somehow returned to a sense of sanity. Weapon sales had been displaced by green technology and products that were designed to be recycled as the biggest dollar earners for all the permanent members of the UN Security Council. That was quite a transition.

Anderson Craig was fully aware he'd been part of big changes that had brought the world back from the brink of disaster. He felt good about what he'd done with a long life, and smiled to himself as Jenny slept; the big car glided silently on, and the miles rolled gently by. He knew that the future was assured for his grandchildren, and their grandchildren's grandchildren.

This all seems unlikely? But that's how things are in the Panglossian province of Pollyanna land!

25

Stuart L. Pimm

Stuart L. Pimm is a conservation biologist whose focus is the study and prevention of species extinctions worldwide. He is the recipient of the Dr. A. H. Heineken Prize in Environmental Sciences from The Royal Netherlands Academy of Arts and Sciences.

LETTERS TO MY GRANDCHILDREN AND GREAT-GRANDCHILDREN

Christmas 2050 at my grandson's house.

"*OK, kid! Grandmother is here. We're all going to watch a movie.*"

"*What movie, Daddy?*"

"*Well, it's more than a hundred years old!*"

"*Wow, what's it called?*"

"The Wizard of Oz."

"*A wizard, Daddy?*"

"*You'll see. And there's a special treat afterwards. Grandmother is going to read a letter. It's from her dad; he wrote it over forty years ago—and just for you and your cousins! So, let's watch, OK?*"

29th April 2007

Girls:

There are two letters in this packet. You only need to read one of them, and I pray it's the second. You'll know which one, and you may even remember my telling you about it in an e-mail (remember them!) all those years ago.

Letter 1

Hey, kids, this is your great-grandfather. You were born after I died, so I could not know you, but I think about you almost every day. I'm that funny-looking old man in photographs next to grandmother in Africa.

What did you think of the movie? There's one part I know you will not understand. It's when Dorothy worries about wild animals—"Lions and tigers and bears. Oh my!" I know you've seen these animals in zoos—they were probably asleep. They haven't been wild animals since before you were born.

There was a time when they were wild. And there were wild places, places where I could travel for days and see only wild things. I wrote this in my diary in India fifty years ago.

Tigers do not roar. Lions roar, so do elephants. In the complete night of the Indian jungle, a tiger moans and makes the forest shake. They sound completely terrifying, for from the sound of their voices, they must be monsters of impossible proportions. As I walk back from eating dinner through the forest clearing to the guest house where I'm staying, I realize that I could be a tiger's dinner!

Gaur are wild cattle, powerfully muscular under their sleek coats. (They are so different from the cows you see in the petting zoo!) Gaur, hidden by the jungle in the day, stroll silently into the clearings as dusk falls, very wild and very threatening, as they appear suddenly in the lights of our car. The bull is huge, his horns no ornament, for the cows that are with him are his alone because he's gored the only slightly less impressive bull who challenged him.

The tiger is not after me. Gaur are tiger food. While my mind tells me that I'm unlikely to be the tiger's supper, the hairs standing up on my neck don't believe it.

I have lion stories, too. In Zambia, we watched a pride of lions taking a long afternoon's sleep. As dusk approached, first one female, then another, woke up, stretched, and set off silently toward a distant group of antelope. We followed at a distance. After it got dark, we could hear the antelope snort, out of fear. Then, a thud, and we turned on the car lights. A lioness had grabbed the male antelope by the neck, pinning it to the ground. In seconds, three other lionesses were in on the kill, then the two males—who'd done nothing until now—came in to claim, well, "the lion's share." In a couple of minutes, nothing was left. Only then did we notice that this was thirty meters from my tent!

I hope you've seen this photograph of me. All you can see is the top of my white safety helmet—along with that of two other people in a small rubber boat—next to a huge blue whale. It was the largest living mammal ever. Before it became extinct, it was an amazing sight, especially when only a few meters away. The photograph is from a helicopter as it hovered above us, a long way off the coast of Mexico.

Did the wild and its animals scare me, as they did Dorothy? No! It was wonderful to be in truly wild places—we just had to be careful.

I once traveled through a part of the Amazon so remote that our only guides were people born in the forest, who still lived in the forest, and we shared their huts. They hunted in the forest, knew how to use its plants. Even fifty years ago, the Amazon was special, for rainforests everywhere in the world were being burned. A little of that forest remains, of course, but it's a lot drier and burns a lot more than it did when I wrote this. Of course, no one lives in the forest anymore.

Only a few very old men still know how to use blow guns and make the darts tipped with curare for hunting. I hope your parents still have the gun and darts that our guide gave me for my helping him fight off the oil companies. We were successful for a while, but the world's ever-increasing need for oil cleared the forest in Ecuador in a few years' time. The forest is gone, the lovely macaws with it, and no one speaks the language of my guide anymore. We knew the oil would only keep cars in the United States running for a few weeks.

We also knew that clearing the forest was particularly stupid, for it put gasses into the air that make the planet hot, when keeping those forests would have soaked up those gasses and kept it cool.

I never saw a polar bear in the wild—but they hunted seals from sea ice that has all but melted. Watching them sleeping in the zoo is not the same thing. (While I'm thinking of it, please do as your parents tell you when you're outside and keep covered up against the sun. Of course, I know it's now far too hot to be outdoors in the summer.)

Countries made national parks fifty years ago, but we knew they were too small even then for lions and tigers. It was obvious that if we didn't make them larger, that species would eventually die out—and they did. It wasn't just the big stuff either. In my day, there were ten thousand kinds of birds and I tried to see all of them! Now, nearly a thousand of them are gone forever—or are so rare that almost no one sees them.

We've done a poor job of saving the wonderful variety of life on Earth and I know that interesting animals and plants are disappearing every year. I had predicted that we'd lose species a thousand times faster than we should; I so wish I had been wrong.

What remains of our planet is not wild, but it's still very special. Do a better job of looking after Earth than I did, kids. You don't want to be writing a letter like this one to *your* great-grandkids in the twenty-second century.

Letter 2

Hey, kids, this is your great-grandfather. You were born after I died, so I could not know you, but I think about you almost every day. I'm that funny-looking old man in photographs next to grandmother in Africa.

This letter is to tell you to not take "no" for an answer! I took your grandmother into her first rainforest at six weeks old, covered in a mosquito net; by the time she was ten, she was helping me in the field. The Amazon is an amazing wilderness, so demand one of those ecotours for your next birthday. Be very respectful of the people there who have chosen to lead traditional lives in the forest.

If your parents haven't taken you tiger watching yet, it's about time. I know you go whale watching all the time. Aren't blue whales spectacular? I was very lucky to see them, for they almost became extinct. Ask for the big trip! Start in South Africa and drive the route that keeps you inside the Southern Africa MegaPark. Go north, across the Zambezi, and keep on going into the Serengeti. If you book early enough, you can stay in camps within the park, with no need to stray outside for the three-week trip.

When the lions are all asleep, have grandmother tell you about how people at the start of this century thought we might lose wild places and the species that lived there. I was one of them. Seems silly now, doesn't it? There's a line or two about it in your history book somewhere, but it won't be on the test.

Remember Dorothy in the movie? There *are* wild animals, so be careful!

26

Malcolm Bricklin

Malcolm Bricklin, founder and CEO of Visionary Vehicles, is recognized as one of the automobile industry's foremost entrepreneurs. He is also the founder of Subaru of America and Yugo America and is currently working on the design, engineering, import, and distribution of a "signature" line of electric cars and light trucks from China into North America.

FUTURE CARS AND THE JETSONS

I have six sons, and it may be that both a large part of what I see for the next fifty years and nearly all of what I have worked on much of my professional life derive from my being in the room when they were young and tuned the television week after week to *The Jetsons.* Interestingly, the show first aired in the 1960s and was supposed to be taking place "100 years into the future," so maybe the timing is just about right.

In transportation, which is where I spend most of my time and thought, I expect to see not in fifty years, but probably in no more than ten, a hybrid car that is completely electric. While the hybrids we drive today alternate between a battery and an internal combustion engine, based on what the computer determines to be the optimum power source, these cars will be totally battery-powered. The purpose of the engine will be to recharge the battery, giving the car greater range and thereby making it a viable choice for daily travel.

The interesting element in this whole scenario is that, if current plans are realized, the car is much more than a source of transportation. If foul weather or downed power lines cut off the electricity in your home, your car becomes an alternate source. What's more, you will be able to plug your car in at night to recharge the battery, using electricity at a time when the grid at your local power plant is least in demand. That means, with the right arrangement, you might buy your power at one rate and sell it back to the city—if you are not using it—during the day at a higher rate. In Austin, Texas, Austin Energy has already taken a step in this direction and will be ready to move when plug-in cars arrive on the scene.

> *You will be able to plug your car in at night to recharge the battery, using electricity at a time when the grid at your local power plant is least in demand.*

Getting those plug-ins to consumers is the priority for me and my colleagues right now, and building the dealer infrastructure will make it happen. Already a number of employers, Google and Bank of America being two cases in point, are offering monetary incentives to employees who drive hybrids. Growing the market and the dealers to deliver the cars is a synergistic process. Once the system is in place, there is no reason to believe the cost per vehicle could not come down dramatically.

Imagine, though, what kind of dealers these will be. As hybrids become modular, rather than your calling for a maintenance appointment, your dealer will have your car and all of its parts reflected in computer data files. You get a call that says, "Hello, it looks as if you need a new Widgetario Number 1318. May we send someone out this afternoon to bring it to you?"

Even better than hybrids, although a bit more futuristic, would be the introduction of flying cars à la George Jetson's bubble-top. I've worked on this for years and am convinced it is viable. Consider only two of what could be several benefits: (1) no need for the construction and maintenance of an elaborate highway system or even bridges over calm water; and (2) optimum time efficiency since we would be able to go "as the crow flies," limited only by whatever restrictions are created for safety purposes.

Much as I like to talk and think about the future in transportation, the other parts of life on Earth I believe will change just as dramatically, but not necessarily always positively.

I'll mention just a few:

- In architecture, I believe we will see the building of structures that are aesthetically magnificent, much like the ones already dotting the skyline in Dubai. Beauty and function will go hand in hand.

- On the global scene, China will be the next economic world power, with India close behind. Where will the United States be? I can't say, but I am most interested to find out not only where the United States will be, but where other "older" economies and cultures will align themselves. I believe staunchly we will end up being better; I just can't quite see where better is yet.

- Rather than talk about education, we will talk about learning. By that I mean that our approach now is to assume that one or another form of education creates a kind of elite segment of society. If, instead, we speak of a "learned" person, it becomes apparent that our society is not differentiated based on access to an institution or a specific educational regimen. What's more, we come to respect the *differences* in our ideas and among ourselves.

- When it comes to health, my view is not nearly so rosy, at least in terms of institutions and organizations that deliver care (or don't, as the case may be). What I do see, though, as the most doable way to address this problem is the growth of a shared value system wherein you and I take responsibility for our own health. In other words, if in the next fifty years, we work on staying healthy as individuals, whatever system we develop to deliver care will have far less to do and therefore be better able to succeed. And at the same time we will be in the best position possible to take advantage of rapidly advancing technology in life extension.

Overall, whatever we drive, however we live, whomever we listen to for ideas and inspiration, we are part of a race that survives.

One more compelling point. I am among those who believe a pandemic is coming. There is no "if"; only when. Accepting that it is a truism that healthy people survive what their sicklier friends cannot.

Overall, whatever we drive, however we live, whomever we listen to for ideas and inspiration, we are part of a race that survives. I have often thought that perhaps the most devastating one event for today's world would be the irretrievable destruction of our computer system. Still, my own parents lived long and well without computers. Fifty years hence there may or may not be differences in speed, comfort, and convenience. Humanity, though, will surely overcome adversity.

27

Abdulla Salem El-Badri

Abdulla Salem El-Badri is secretary general of the Organization of the Petroleum Exporting Countries (OPEC).

A WORLD WITHOUT BORDERS

I foresee a world without borders.

Developments in the world today are preparing the ground for a major demographic change, which will become very visible some fifty years from now. I foresee a world where none of today's developed countries can retain their homogeneity as the influx of immigrants—with different cultures, lifestyles, religions, etc.—into these countries impacts on their indigenous cultures. This trend has already started and it is only going to increase.

While the developed nations offer better living conditions, most of them have manpower shortages, thus pulling migrants to them. At the same time, life in the less-developed countries has continued to become harsher, pushing able-bodied people to migrate in search of greener pastures.

A point in time will come when authorities of developed countries, especially those with relatively small populations, will become concerned about the dilution of their cultures and take steps to stop it. However, they will not succeed because, in the next fifty years, national authorities are likely to become less powerful over their citizens and other residents of their countries as the concept of humanity breaks down national boundaries. This can, of course, be attributed to the enduring argument about new technologies in communications, etc.—should the countries of the world keep their traditions and standards of living in their own territories, or should they let them fly across the globe?

I foresee all people having dual citizenships—that of their nation-state and that of the world. The world will come to the rescue of its citizens when their national sovereigns abuse their human rights.

28

Lee H. Hamilton

Lee H. Hamilton is director of the Woodrow Wilson International Center for Scholars and the Center on Congress at Indiana University. He was vice-chair of the 9/11 Commission and co-chair of the Iraq Study Group. He served for thirty-four years in the United States Congress and chaired the House Committees on Foreign Affairs and Intelligence.

TECHNOLOGY, SECURITY, AND LIBERTY IN 50 YEARS

It has been nearly 150 years since Abraham Lincoln stood at Gettysburg and posed a question that defined our civil war and our national purpose: whether a nation, "conceived in Liberty, and dedicated to the proposition that all men are created equal . . . can long endure." Fifty years from today, new and unprecedented stresses to the United States will imbue that question with renewed relevance.

Revolutionary advances in technology will continue at a pace we cannot imagine. If we look around today from the perspective of fifty years ago, many things have not changed. We still drive automobiles powered by the internal combustion engine, generate much of our electricity with steam power, and take aspirin (patented in 1899) when we have a headache. Yet the information equivalent of the Library of Congress is now generated every fifteen minutes.

The information revolution has changed education, medicine, commerce, warfare, politics, and even our dating habits. When we add the biotech revolution and the new nanotechnology revolution to advances in telecommunications and computing, we have the building blocks for transformative change.

Governments and corporations will have an enormous capacity to collect and manage information. So will individuals. This will open the door to limitless opportunities, but it will also have a dark side: it will be increasingly difficult for the United States—or any collection of governments and corporations—to monopolize the world's most dangerous technologies. How we govern and safeguard technology, and protect our privacy and liberties, will be a preeminent challenge for the United States and humankind.

The diffusion of technology will be only one of the centrifugal challenges facing America. The population of the United States will be substantially larger and more diverse, with huge influxes of immigrants from Asia and, principally, Latin America. We cannot halt this change. The American economy will continue to create jobs that cannot be filled by native-born workers, thus we will continue to turn to immigrants. How we employ, regulate, and integrate this steady influx— which will surely lead to an America that is far more Hispanic—will be a priority for governments from the town hall to the Congress.

Abroad, the relative position of the United States will decline, though democracy and free market economics will expand. America will continue to be the world's preeminent power, but the absolute post-Cold War military, economic, and cultural dominance cannot hold. China will challenge our economic strength and will surely play a more assertive diplomatic and military role in Asia. A united Europe, a rising India, an assertive Russia, and a resilient Japan will represent other poles of power. So will new regional powers like Brazil, South Africa, Indonesia, and a potentially unified Korea. To adapt to this change and to be effective, international institutions like the United Nations will have to be substantially reformed, if not rebuilt.

Similarly, global culture will become more diffuse. Americans are accustomed to having the world's greatest athletes coming here to play pro sports; having our movies and television programs dominate global entertainment; hearing English spoken around the world; and having foreign students flood our universities. While our culture will continue to be preeminent, emerging powers will have increasing influence. Chinese will be spoken in boardrooms and intercontinental hotels and will become the language of the Internet for tens of millions. Huge markets like China and India will support larger manufacturing, service, entertainment, and athletic industries. International students will seek a broad range of locations to study.

Chinese will be spoken in boardrooms and intercontinental hotels and will become the language of the Internet for tens of millions.

The United States will continue to grapple with the security threats we face today. Terrorism will persist, and there will almost certainly be more attacks on American soil. Our relationship with the Islamic world will continue to be a challenge, though that relationship will deepen beyond our current reliance on a few key governments like Egypt, Saudi Arabia, and Pakistan. Proliferation of weapons of mass destruction will occupy more and more of our time. Our most important bilateral relationship in the world will be with China. How we manage that relationship will largely determine whether the world's great powers continue to manage disputes within an international system, or whether we return to the tradition of great power conflict.

Yet the principal security threats in fifty years may be attributed not to armies or terrorists but to the environment. Because of environmental degradation, population growth, and climate change, there will be unprecedented strains on the most basic resources: water and food. Over a quarter of a billion people could be displaced by famine in fifty years. Unless the international community takes assertive action, horrible conflicts will be fought in the most environmentally vulnerable regions—Africa, the Middle East, and Southern Asia. The instability wrought by these conflicts—and the potentially irreversible damage of ocean pollution, over-farming, urbanization, and carbon emissions—could lead to a drop in the standard of living worldwide.

These forces present critical questions for America. How can we make use of technology without permitting it to erode our liberties or empower our enemies? How can we adjust to sustained immigration while upholding our laws and national cohesion? How can we reform the international system and renew our global leadership in a more multipolar world? How will we manage our two most volatile relationships—with China and with the Islamic world? How can we reconcile economic and population growth with the absolute necessity to protect our planet and develop new sources of energy? Can our nation, so conceived, so dedicated, still endure and prevail?

The bottom line is that the United States will shape its own future and still play the leading role in shaping the world's. Our political framework, the Constitution, if properly understood and used, is sufficiently flexible and ingenious to adjust to these fast-changing realities. The technological revolution is largely the product of American know-how. The change that will sweep the world will continue to be grounded in American values—democratic governance and free market economics. As that change provokes swelling turmoil, our country will be tested. Our nation and our system will endure—but only if Americans rise to the challenge.

29

Steven Beckwith

Steven Beckwith is an astronomer and director of the Space Telescope Science Institute at Johns Hopkins University, which runs the science operations for the Hubble Space Telescope.

OUR PLACE IN THE UNIVERSE

Although we cannot foresee just *how* we will change our lives in fifty years, we already have a pretty good idea of how we will react to the changes. For most of us, or more accurately, most of our children's children, life will be easier and intellectually richer in fifty years. Our tools for dealing with everyday needs will be better and more efficient, and they will reduce the most frightening of life's uncertainties. Gene manipulation and the use of drugs will cure many of today's most debilitating diseases and will replace low-tech procedures such as surgery with the incredible ease of pill or injections, thus greatly reducing the fuss of medicine. Life spans will increase, discomfort from chronic problems will decrease, and the overall cost of well-being will come down, removing us even further from the pain and uncertainty that have always accompanied life. To be sure, the majority of the world's population will face difficult living conditions, but even those conditions will improve, on average.

We will know much, much more about nature, the universe, and our own origins. Unfortunately, we will not be any wiser in using this knowledge to cure society's ills. Looking back from the middle of the twenty-first century, we will wonder how so much knowledge can enlighten us and at the same time be so difficult to use to improve the social condition. The clash between knowledge and belief, best seen today in debates about evolution versus biblical creation, will be as strong as it is now despite enormous progress in understanding the mechanisms by which we were created. Advances in cognitive science will reveal that many of our most controversial behaviors—tribalism, violence, even sexual preference—have deep roots in biology and will not be eliminated by social reform. But these advances will face barriers to their use for improving society: resistance to the concentrated power needed for "scientific" social reform and (more powerfully) the need for religious certainty that makes it

The prospects for discovering intelligent life elsewhere will be very good, prompting a renewed interest in space science as the best way to find our nearest neighbors.

difficult to give up our long-held prejudices about human behavior and the best ways to regulate its worst excesses. I fear that new technology will only enable more of the anti-social violence that seems to be a constant plague on otherwise free societies.

Looking outward, we will realize that life on Earth is not very special and our species is not fundamentally different from all the others on this planet. We will have strong but not quite irrefutable evidence for life around other stars just as we now have strong but not quite irrefutable evidence for water on other bodies in the solar system, a much smaller step. This evidence will remove any intellectual foundation for the notion that the earth is a special place in the universe and mark the end of the current era in the same way that Copernicus's (correct) treatise marked the end of the last one.

Most of us will continue to believe we are special and will act accordingly. Some religions will adjust, but most will ignore the mounting evidence for our pedestrian role in the cosmos. The prospects for discovering intelligent life elsewhere will be very good, prompting a renewed interest in space science as the best way to find our nearest neighbors.

This last advance will be the most interesting to me, if I am still alive. At least one advanced society (I suspect it will not be the United States) will recognize the enormous difficulty of space travel, especially with humans, and the relative ease of long-distance communication, and pursue its exploration with telescopes and remote sensors; most countries currently invest in the hope that long-distance space travel will become easy. This society will build new satellites to receive signals from the universe and work out the best way to transmit terrestrial information to distant planets. Barring some happy accident, it will be too early to have discovered other sentient beings, but we will have a pretty good idea how to do so and make it happen in the fifty years to follow. And more than our ability to put people in space or to walk on the moon, that first discovery of extraterrestrial beings will mark the beginning of the era in which humans expand their horizon beyond the pale blue dot we call home.

30

Tim Mack

Tim Mack is president of The World Future Society, a non-profit, non-partisan scientific and educational association of people interested in how social and technological developments are shaping the future.

SNAPSHOT OF A WORLD WITH THE NEW NATION OF CALIFORNIA

Let's take a snapshot of the world of 2058. Assume we live in California, which is now a separate nation, after its secession from the United States. It is not a big surprise, considering its history, that California never lost its rather unique Mexican/Spanish heritage. The coastline we are standing upon is the same one that California has had for the past several centuries. Thankfully, the "Big One" has never occurred, and the damaging earthquakes of the twentieth century are a thing of the past. The San Andreas Fault is now part of an E-monitoring system that tracks pressures along the eight hundred miles of fault lines up to ten miles down that can defuse internal pressures as they develop. Other digital worlds, subsequent generations of Second Life, are as fully functional as the "real world," and insurance companies now offer coverage for digital property—after enough celebrities acquired real estate in digital worlds—and this insurance segment long ago exceeded a trillion Euros in valuation.

As we look out to the Pacific, the scene can best be described as cluttered. The shoreline is no longer pristine but populated with a wide range of floating and anchored habitats, wind power stations, tidal current generators, and artificial islands. These and numerous other alternative energy sources have addressed the limitations set by the decades-old total California ban on fossil fuels. People still have cars—far too many everywhere in the world— but in California they don't run on gasoline or anything combustible unless you live way out in the country. Everyone seems to want to benefit from the sea or live on it, especially after the water crisis of the 2030s made H_2O such a valuable commodity. The technological miracle that synthesizes water from air has made all the difference, but people are still crazy about the ocean. But since seashore real estate is no longer affordable by anyone but large corporations, it is no wonder digital property has become so popular.

This mid-century scene is a relatively peaceful one, although a few decades back it would not have been. There were endless riots in the criminally overcrowded cities, and what were called the SARS Wars, with its constantly mutating diseases, had the world scared silly—until the global ban on biotech weapons became fully effective. While the cities are not too much better now, the world-wide population decline has taken some of the pressure off, and migration back to rural settings is becoming the norm. What few conflicts that are still fought are largely in a digital world. Unmanned aircraft still patrol real canyons and real cities. Their missiles are real, and they occasionally kill real people. But their pilots sit in virtual reality (VR) rooms half a world away from danger.

Now, much of human imagination goes into redesigning our own bodies. As nearly all of the life-threatening diseases have been overcome, the modern focus is personal accessories. People can replace their own retinas with artifi-

> *The shoreline is no longer pristine but populated with a wide range of floating and anchored habitats, wind power stations, tidal current generators, and artificial islands.*

cial ones, not only to improve sharpness, brightness, and resolution, but to switch between several modes of input. The "reality" mode (it's a neural switch, so you just think "real") brings you the images from the physical world surrounding your body, while the VR mode lets you interact with any other world (depicted or imagined), such as viewing your daughter playing in her kindergarten classroom or your mother in her nursing home. VR mode allows you to be some place you're physically not or in several places at once. And as these technologies have matured, personal upgrade options once just for the rich have become commonplace. Education and research have been popular applications of the digital retina for visiting E-worlds. Of course, this has completely changed education, for both children and adults. A field trip in biology class can now be a trip inside a tree, moving through microscopic vessels, visiting the end of a branch and watching food and light turn into a new leaf.

Digital technology has brought virtual reality to life in a new universe of human understanding. Today, in 2058, if we want to understand the depths of our own bodies and minds, we go digital. Humans are too complex to understand themselves otherwise. We are on the road to attain a new level of complexity, one where body and mind meet on the common playground of information-carrying energy. Traditional male skills of strength, logic, and the delivery of DNA were valued throughout our human history. Digital technology took away the monopoly on all three, because technology often did a better job (except for perhaps the third one). Over time, traditional female qualities such as caring and intuition have replaced strength and logic on the cutting edge of innovation. What we don't know in 2058 is what shape the next "version" of humanity will take and who will guide those changes. In the past, we often wondered about the genes each of us owns, but now we wonder who owns our genes.

Now, we can build creatures, living and non-living, from the bottom up.

We have penetrated nature to arrive at the common ground where matter meets information; where information technology meets molecular technology and turns one into the other. Now, we can build creatures, living and nonliving, from the bottom up. This is all complemented by the ability to put together the details of one's own life, genotype, phenotypic details, experiences, and the emotions that went along with them for a range of purposes, from therapy to art. A personal avatar keeps all of the pictures you ever took and the music ever played, stores medical history and the 3D kinematics of muscles and limbs, tracks daily diet, blood-pressure, and what was said on the first date. Indeed, intelligent machines have learned a lot, but they still trail humans in imagination and intuition, and lack the force of curiosity, as they never get bored with the status quo. Otherwise, the machines do many things better than we do, including dancing, although they tend to repeat themselves in the way they express emotional gestures. The ability of the human mind to go beyond the status quo and believe in dreams has proved a cornerstone of our humanity.

During the first half of the twenty-first century, we saw a new emerging class of challenges that were no longer hierarchical but complex in nature. That is, no one of them was dramatically more important than the others, but all had to be addressed as a system. They were fast-developing, evolving, interactive, and often nonlinear, where seemingly small events led to substantial results. These new types of problems could not be met with any single solution, as they seldom stayed solved, but required instead continuous and ongoing management.

This does not mean all problems have disappeared. Total urbanization appeared at one time to be unavoidable, and countries like Turkey have passed the 90 percent mark. This situation was not improved by nearly 150 million automobiles worldwide, most of them in cities. But smaller, more flexible and independent countries like California made tough decisions and pulled back from the edge. While urban overcrowding, too many cars (nearly two-thirds in what used to be called the developing world), and the world's seemingly endless appetite for energy continue to trouble us, there is more of a feeling that solutions are possible, that corporations won't end up owning the entire world, and that human imagination is still the most powerful force in the universe. If China can pull back from its nearly catastrophic environmental and resource crisis, then humans can do anything.

31

Marian Wright Edelman

*Marian Wright Edelman is founder and president of the Children's Defense
Fund (CDF), the nation's strongest independent voice for children and
families. She was the first black woman admitted to the Mississippi Bar,
where she directed the NAACP Legal Defense and Educational Fund.
Honors include the Presidential Medal of Freedom, a MacArthur
Foundation Prize Fellowship, and the Robert F. Kennedy Lifetime
Achievement Award for her writings, which include eight books.*

OUR CHILDREN, OUR FUTURE

How will we be fifty years from today? That will depend on the choices we
make today. Eleanor Roosevelt said, "Tomorrow is now." I've spent most of my
life focused on ensuring every child the healthy and safe foundation they need
to make it to successful adulthood with the help of caring families and communities. But all children and families are affected by the policies of our nation
and the values of our culture. Too often, our policies and cultural values do
not support healthy child and family development.

Although we live in an era of stunning intellectual, technological, and scientific achievement, have sent humans to the Moon, spaceships to Mars, cracked
the genetic code, amassed tens of billions of dollars from a tiny microchip,
learned how to transmit information faster than we can digest it, and discovered

cures for diseases that give hope to millions, billions of people live and die from poverty. With more just choices and moral leadership, we could usher in a great period in human history—one that closes the growing gap between rich and poor and adheres to a concept of enough for every human being in our nation and world.

Despite unprecedented material wealth in the United States, we allow nearly thirteen million children to live in poverty and nine million to go without health insurance. The majority live in working families. The United States leads the world in health technology, millionaires and billionaires, military expenditures, and Gross Domestic Product but lags behind most of the industrialized world in infant mortality and low birthweight rates, children killed by guns, and the gap between rich and poor. How do we build the spiritual and political will to use our extraordinary resources to shape a more just society at home and peaceful rather than war-torn tomorrow in our world? How do we change the unbearable dissonance between promise and performance; between good politics and good policy; between professed and practiced human and family values; between racial and religious creed and racial and religious deed; between calls for community and rampant individualism and greed; and between our capacity to prevent and alleviate human deprivation and disease and our political and spiritual will to do so?

We must reset our moral compass if we are to build a world fit for our children over the next fifty years and if humankind is to progress rather than regress.

As we move through the first decade of a new century and millennium, we have been given an incredible opportunity and responsibility to think differently, even radically, about the kind of nation and world we want to build for our children and their children. I believe women, especially mothers and grandmothers, must catalyze and lead the movement.

At home, we must insist that our nation commit to guaranteeing health coverage for every child and to making child poverty history in America over the next decade. As a global community, we must make it a priority to stop the morally intolerable, relentless, and preventable loss of millions of mothers' and children's lives. A mother dies from childbirth every minute, and millions more mothers suffer lifelong disabilities each year. Over 14.4 million mothers and children under age five die each year from mostly preventable causes. And 100 million school-age children do not go to school. Fifty-five percent of them are girls who need to be empowered through education.

These facts are not acts of God. They are our human choices. They can and must be changed. But it will take powerful women joining together across race, culture, income, faith, age, and discipline raising a mighty and sustained voice for powerless women and children. Eleanor Roosevelt believed that only powerful women would protect powerless women and that a woman's will is the strongest thing in the world.

That will can and must redefine progress and success over the next fifty years and make sure that compassion trumps consumption, justice triumphs over greed, and community values prevail over selfish individualism. Our children are the transforming and unifying metaphor for a new era. If the child is safe, everyone is safe. Every prophet, president, king, queen, leader, and human being of every place, color, gender, and faith entered life as a baby. The child is the present and the future and our Creator's universal messenger of hope and immortality. It's time for the world to get it and to save millions of children's lives being ravaged by the wars, neglect, abuse, and racial, ethnic, religious, and class divisions of adults. Protecting today's children—tomorrow's leaders and parents—is the moral and commonsense litmus test of our humanity. How we meet that test will define how we measure up in fifty years.

32

Valli Moosa

Valli Moosa is president of The World Conservation Union (IUCN), the world's largest conservation network. The union brings together 83 states, 110 government agencies, more than eight hundred non-governmental organizations, and ten thousand scientists and experts from 181 countries in an effort to influence, encourage, and assist societies to conserve the integrity and diversity of nature and to ensure that any use of natural resources is equitable and ecologically sustainable.

LANDSCAPES AND LIVING CONDITIONS

After over fifty years of social upheaval, personal and diplomatic efforts, and an energy revolution based on solar technologies, we have finally managed to stabilize climate change. However, landscapes and living conditions have altered irrevocably, and old world maps from 2007 are unrecognizable.

The global community is currently finalizing agreements on new national boundaries after the extensive melting of glaciers and ice sheets, new river systems, and rising sea levels inundated low-lying islands and coastal areas, and flooded huge areas of Asia and the Pacific. The expense of maintaining sea defenses in parts of North America and Europe eventually proved too high, and parts of London and New York are now permanently under water.

Looking back, it is clear that in the early 2000s, governments were unprepared for the massive disruptions that the changing weather would have on everyday life. The dustbowls, forest fires, and droughts in Australia and the American Midwest, and the flooding of water, sewage, and energy utilities in Europe and Asia, wreaked havoc in peoples' lives, creating widespread migrations and conflicts in the 2020s. Despite all disruption, people have been pretty adaptable and have learned to adjust to harsher and more unpredictable living conditions.

The world failed to meet its earlier target to halt the loss of biodiversity by 2010, and thousands of plant and animal species went extinct due to climate change in the 2020s, imperiling our basic life-support systems. But thanks to radical advances in gene-bank technology, molecular engineering, and assisted migration, we finally managed to reverse the human-induced loss of biodiversity by the year 2030, and there is now a continuous system of biodiversity corridors connecting fauna and flora across ecosystems.

There is less public concern about manipulating life-forms these days, due to the dramatic loss of biodiversity and food resources, but all new projects are reviewed by ethics groups with representatives from science, business, and civil society. Despite some amazing breakthroughs and the co-creation of Nature v.2, we still haven't learned how to recreate "life" itself though.

The old oil-based economy has more or less faded away, along with its associated power structures and dynamics. This is one of the reasons why the old Western civilization rapidly declined after the 2020s. Countries and companies that managed to leapfrog to new energy and business models in the first couple of decades of the new millennium are now thriving, with the new generation of multinationals based in China, India, Brazil, and Southern Africa.

There have been significant advances in governance systems. The flawed reforms of fifty years ago provoked the breakdown of the older United Nations system just after 2012, but a new multilateral system emerged based on a three-chamber system of collaborative governance between representatives of governments, business, and civil society. Africa is now a well-established United States of Africa, with one economy and a continental governance system.

The population in 2058 is not as high as was predicted at the start of the millennium due to widespread pandemics, which are now under control. Compared to the early twenty-first century all countries have a much better standard of living, although there are still pockets of deprivation in parts of the United States. The decline of the oil-based economy transformed the old industrial agricultural systems, and a revolution in renewable energies has allowed more local, diversified, and decentralized resource systems to evolve.

Based on the early experiments in the carbon trade, markets exist for all of nature's services, including soil, water, air (carbon and other elements), solar radiation, and pollination. Income raised through these trading mechanisms is going towards planetary ecological restoration schemes. Ecological economics has evolved as a major discipline with full ecological accounting in global and accounting systems. Sustainable development was strengthened when consumption patterns came under the control of a new globally binding treaty that froze exploitation and use of materials to 2020 levels.

Sustainable development was strengthened when consumption patterns came under the control of a new globally binding treaty that froze exploitation and use of materials to 2020 levels.

The major paradigm shift of this millennium has been the industrial revolution based on ideas generated at the interface between biology and engineering. The key breakthrough came when researchers learned how to mimic the energy-chemistry of green plants, which convert carbon dioxide and water, in the presence of sunlight, into oxygen and energy, and construct new energy flow and storage facilities based on plant biochemistry and structure. There has been a major discovery that, with a bit of human help, nature can actually heal itself and cleanup the messes we have created.

The traditional "take-make-and-waste" production and consumption systems of the late twentieth century have been replaced by cradle-to-cradle systems and service-flow models. Everything is reused and recycled as in nature itself. One person's waste is someone else's resource. We no longer buy products such as lightbulbs or carpets, but rather lighting and flooring "services." All manufacturers are responsible for recycling their products, organized through networks of recycling entrepreneurs.

Nanotechnology developed quickly at the start of the new millennium, giving rise to molecular manufacturing and desktop manufacturing. In 2058, we can now download three-dimensional blueprints to produce simple solid products from nanoassemblers at home. With radical advances in light technologies, you rarely see the old-fashioned desktop computers with screens anymore. We have been able to access global information and online shopping through our mobile phones and household appliances for years.

We are currently experiencing a Renaissance in China and Africa. Thanks to the Internet and development of new social networks, new models of democracy have taken root in China and a new wave of practical Chinese philosophies and wisdom has become fashionable worldwide. Mandarin overtook English as the lingua franca when the old empire went into decline in the 2020s. Africa is a thriving continent today and the center of modern cultural expression. It has shown the way on a new relationship between humans and nature, and like China, has become a trendsetter in new eco-friendly technologies.

With advances in education and communications, most people are much more aware of their collective impact on the environment than they used to be. The role of nature as part of a human life-support system is much better understood. It has finally dawned on people that they are integral parts of living ecosystems, and that whatever they do to the earth, air, or water, they are ultimately doing to themselves.

Religious fundamentalism throughout the world has waned thanks again to the rise of global communications and a new spirit of cooperation that emerged after the pandemics. More extreme groups are objects of curiosity rather than a danger to society. A shift in human consciousness has generated a creative fusion of spirituality and science that has transformed medical research and healthcare. In 2058, we have developed a more holistic view of our multidimensional selves.

33

Leon E. Panetta and
James D. Watkins

*The Honorable Leon E. Panetta and Admiral James D. Watkins are
co-chairs of the Joint Ocean Commission Initiative.*

*Leon E. Panetta served as chief of staff for President Clinton and was
chairman of the Pew Oceans Commission. He is also director of the Leon
& Sylvia Panetta Institute for Public Policy, California State University at
Monterey Bay.*

*Admiral James D. Watkins's forty-year naval career culminated in
attaining the Navy's highest uniformed office, chief of naval operations.
He is a former secretary of energy.*

Go Green by Thinking Blue

The United States is experiencing an environmental awakening—it's been
called the "greening" of America. We are increasingly aware that the long-term
strength of the economy, our personal well-being, and our quality of life are
closely linked to the health of the planet, which in turn hinges on the health
of the oceans that cover over 70 percent of the earth's surface. The oceans regulate our weather, feed us, and provide us with much of the air we breathe, all

while contributing $138 billion to the American economy each year. For America to really go green we need to think blue. This means expanding our environmental focus to include the health of our oceans and making decisions about managing the oceans that take into account all of the elements of this extraordinarily interrelated and complex system.

Thinking blue comes pretty naturally to us. Leon grew up along the coast in Monterey, California, a town where most families had deep connections to the fishing industry, either as fishermen, cannery workers, or small business owners in a town where the economy was entirely dependent on the fishing industry. When overfishing depleted the sardine population to the point of collapse, families who lost their livelihood were devastated. Leon witnessed firsthand the results of the tragic impacts of failing to think blue, and it was this lesson that instilled in him a commitment to protecting the oceans.

The Admiral, a graduate of the Naval Academy, a submariner, and later the Chief of Naval Operations, has spent most of his life near, on, or under the ocean. He recalls a period of our history, notably during the Cold War, when thinking blue was standard operating procedure in the United States. With the country on guard against Soviet missile threats, the nation invested in vital research to understand more about the physical processes in the ocean, giving birth to modern oceanography. However, with the end of the Cold War, our national commitment to studying the oceans faded. Now we are facing new challenges from climate change, pollution, and overexploitation of ocean resources that are also threatening our way of life. The only effective way to respond to these challenges is by thinking blue.

We know there are real problems plaguing our oceans and coasts today. Massive dead zones have formed in the Gulf of Mexico, Chesapeake Bay, and off the coast of Oregon. Overfishing is rapidly depleting fish populations. Daily contamination of beaches makes them unfit for swimming and fishing, which has a dramatic impact on coastal economies that depend on tourism to thrive. Imagine how much revenue a coastal vacation town loses in just one day when the beach is closed at the height of the summer tourist season. In 2005 alone there were more than twenty-thousand such closures and advisories. And most alarming, the acidification of ocean waters is harming coral reefs that support over 25 percent of the ocean's plant and animal population, including microscopic plankton that generate most of the oxygen we need to live.

While these problems are severe, they are also solvable. Efforts to revive depleted fish populations, such as striped bass and shad, have had considerable success. Even in Monterey Bay, through careful management, we've been able to bring back the sardines. Cities and farms around the country are taking steps to prevent human waste and agricultural pollution from contaminating beaches, bays, and rivers, which bolster coastal economies and also help plant and animal life flourish.

These solutions are a good start. If as a nation we follow their lead by committing to think blue, in fifty years we can witness a beautiful new sea change in our oceans that will look like this:

First, there will literally be more fish in the sea. Stocks of severely depleted big fish, such as tuna, billfish, and sharks; crabs in the Chesapeake Bay; abalone in the waters off California; and red snapper in the Gulf of Mexico, will have rebounded to healthy levels. The result is that future generations will be able to enjoy the ocean's bountiful seafood. And the family fisherman—long on the endangered list in New England and along the Gulf Coast—will survive and flourish as an important part of our American heritage and also as a valuable economic anchor that helps coastal communities to thrive.

The sea change will not just mean more fish, but also that the ocean's most iconic and threatened species, including the great whales, seals, sea lions, sea otters, and manatees, will grow in numbers.

The sea change will not just mean more fish, but also that the ocean's most iconic and threatened species, including the great whales, seals, sea lions, sea otters, and manatees, will grow in numbers. The sight of a whale spouting and breeching off the coast of Maine or in the Pacific is awe inspiring. It is something that we want our great-grandchildren to have the opportunity to see for them-selves, not just on a video or in a book.

The sea change will also bring important advances for our coasts and the communities that reside near the shore. By thinking blue, we will curb pollution from agricultural and urban runoff, so that areas such as the Gulf of Mexico, Maine, and Alaska, along with the Chesapeake, Delaware, Tampa, and San Francisco Bays, are able to heal and again serve as vital spawning, nursery, and feeding grounds critical for the growth of juvenile fish and shellfish populations. This also means fewer beach closures, more sandcastles, and safer swimming for those who live in or visit coastal areas. And it means healthier coastal economies that increasingly depend on beach tourism for their livelihood.

While the sea change cannot halt the development of ocean-born hurri-canes and other severe storms, it will mean that the impact of these storms on coastal communities is lessened. By adopting strong building codes and set-back policies, there will be greater buffers between the ocean and homes, and more green space to divert rising water away from property. The result will be that when the next Hurricane Charley or Katrina comes ashore, our coastal cities and towns will be safer and more resilient.

The sea change will mean that we are better equipped to fight threats to human life, from debilitating diseases to climate change. Gone are the days of using leeches to heal disease. Now the oceans hold the promise of cutting-edge treatments or even cures to the most debilitating diseases currently fac-ing us, including cancer and Alzheimer's. Microbes found in ocean sediment have the potential to create new antibiotics, especially important as many infections are becoming increasingly drug resistant. Snails and sponges have been found to contain compounds used in new painkillers and anticancer drugs. But 95 percent of our oceans remain unexplored, and new plant and animal species with medicinal use are waiting to be discovered. By thinking blue we will be protecting the health of our oceans and preserving the vast biodiversity that it harbors, resulting in saved lives and an enhanced quality of life for our great-grandchildren.

Climate change is a global disease that arguably poses an even greater threat to human life. The oceans drive climate change, because they absorb and transport enormous amounts of heat and carbon dioxide. Unfortunately, while this buffering role reduces the impacts of climate change, it is harming the oceans by changing the acid levels and temperature of the water. To fight climate change, we need the best science possible. The sea change will ensure that the oceans are "wired" with a network of sensors and buoys that communicate with satellites monitoring physical, biological, and chemical changes, providing us with important data on how the oceans work and how they are changing. As a result, policymakers will be able to make better-informed decisions about how to respond to climate change.

It is up to all of us to make this sea change happen. We cannot go green without thinking blue—and we cannot keep our oceans healthy without policies that take into account all of the interrelated factors that impact the oceans. By thinking blue, we can ensure that no town is ever again devastated by the collapse of the fishing industry, as Leon witnessed in Monterey Bay growing up. And we can renew our national commitment to getting the scientific information we need to make good decisions about protecting our ocean resources, addressing climate change, strengthening coastal economies, and ensuring our national security.

Americans need to recognize that our individual and collective behavior must change if we are to protect and enhance what is one of greatest legacies we can provide to future generations, a healthy planet. A key step toward fulfilling this legacy is to put a comprehensive national ocean policy in place. We need to take what we know from science and use it to improve and sustain the health of the water, the plants, the fish, the coastal areas, the humans that depend on the oceans, and all the relationships between those pieces of the ocean puzzle. Without a holistic and balanced policy, the sea change we envision will remain beyond our grasp. But we can make it a reality and ensure healthy oceans for future generations—we just need to think blue.

34

Aaron Ciechanover

Dr. Aaron Ciechanover, a Distinguished Research Professor at Technion-Israel Institute of Technology, was awarded the Nobel Prize for Chemistry in 2004 for his work with two other scientists in discovering ubiquitin-mediated protein degradation. This discovery creates an opportunity to develop more effective drugs against cervical cancer, cystic fibrosis, and other diseases.

THE PARADOX

I see a mixed picture when I contemplate the world of fifty years from today. Life will be better in many ways for those in the developed world, while it will likely stay the same or continue to worsen for those in the developing world. And there will be major challenges to the very survival of humanity—challenges that must be met by the developed world.

Rapid advances in the biomedical sciences will bring about benefits in human health and welfare for those living in the developed world. Scientists' understanding of the mechanisms of such serious illnesses as Alzheimer's and many forms of cancer will enable us to develop drugs that will successfully treat these diseases. Unlike the general treatments of today, these drugs will be tailored to the specific genetic repertoire of the patients, ensuring high rates of therapeutic success.

As in the past, when the developing world did not share the world's wealth, life in these countries will continue to be difficult. Africa will continue to be decimated by wars, poverty, malnutrition, and disease. This extreme inequality is the soil on which terror, dictatorships, and religious extremism flourish, and therefore must be addressed by the developed countries, for their own sake.

Much of the suffering we will see in Africa and throughout the developing world in fifty years is not inevitable. Many of the problems could be solved, or greatly alleviated, if the developed world cared enough to focus on developing and funding solutions to the problems. After all, we do understand agriculture, nutrition, and the basics of health care. The knowledge is there; what's not there is the will. Consequently, neither is the funding. I am not optimistic that the developed world will devote significant resources to bringing about a healthy Africa.

Africa will continue to be decimated by wars, poverty, malnutrition, and disease.

The developing world and the developed world together face problems that must be resolved if humanity is to have a sustainable future. Global warming is perhaps the most serious problem—a man-made phenomenon that must also be solved by humankind.

We have developed alternative forms of energy. Paradoxically, the rapid progress in science and technology that has brought so many benefits to humankind is also largely responsible for the damage we witness on our planet; in just a matter of decades we have consumed most of the fossil oil that took nature hundreds of millions of years to form.

Other challenges we face have also been created by the very advances that have yielded great new possibilities. For example, so much will soon be known about a person even before birth that we will be able to predict his or her predisposition to heart disease, mental illness, and a range of other maladies. We may even be able to know, before birth, a great deal about a person's talents and personality. What a challenge to use such knowledge ethically! In certain hands—some governments, insurance companies, and corporations—the knowledge could easily be misused. And how should ethics guide parents who want to ensure that their future children have certain characteristics but not others?

While I am not optimistic that we in the developed world possess the will or the wisdom to successfully address the ethical and other major challenges that we are bequeathing to the next generation, I do not want to lose sight of the richness of life.

There are so many wonders to appreciate and enjoy! The human brain has created so much that is beautiful—great paintings, architecture, music, and literature. Then there are the miracles of nature that stir our sense of awe. Those lucky enough to live in an open society will probably be able to continue enjoying these riches in fifty years. For such people, life is not only challenging; it is also fun.

So how do we bring about a world where the riches of life are shared by all humanity, where they are not limited to the lucky—those relatively few who happen to live in the developed world? Education is the answer. All good things emanate from it. If young people are educated well, they will be citizens of the world, able to understand its challenges, knowing what is needed to address them. Such people will turn their backs on terror and extremism and will direct their talents and knowledge toward changing their own countries and benefiting all of humanity.

35

Elias A. Zerhouni

Elias A. Zerhouni, MD, is director of the National Institutes of Health, the nation's medical research agency.

THE TRANSFORMATION

Midway through the twenty-first century, if we are fortunate, the power of the life sciences will be on the way to being realized in much the way the physical sciences had been for the previous century. Mastery of the biological world will impact not only health but also the ability for humans to develop sensitive solutions to environmental and energy challenges. The future, I hope, will see the life sciences realizing their promise over the next fifty years.

At the beginning of this era, we have been priming the canvas for a different image of medicine, medicine that is *predictive, personalized, preemptive,* and *participatory*. For decades we have known more and more about disease processes, but we have been intervening too late in that process. In recent years, and through intensive research, we have taken diseases that used to be fatal and moved them into survivable, but chronic, conditions. One of the greatest challenges facing our society today that will influence our national competitiveness is the unsustainable growth of health-care expenditures. We are moving into the future with a financial burden that is unparalleled. Despite medical progress, health-care costs in the United States have risen to more than $2 trillion, or about 16 percent of the Gross Domestic Product

(GDP), and they grow at a rate greater than the GDP. The average amount spent yearly on health care per person is about $7,100 today.

To put this in perspective, we need to contrast that escalating cost with our investment in biomedical research. We have learned to diminish the impact of many diseases and disabilities for all Americans over the past thirty years. Americans have gained more than six years of life expectancy, are controlling chronic diseases like diabetes, and are reducing the dreaded complications of blindness and end-stage kidney disease. Americans are aging with better health than ever before. New industries have led to the creation of thousands of companies in the life sciences with impact beyond human health.

In February 2007, the National Heart, Lung, and Blood Institute of the NIH announced that the number of women who die from heart disease has shifted from 1 in 3 to 1 in 4. The mortality rates of cancer, the second leading cause of death in the United States, have been steadily falling.

Treatment for cognitive decline and mental disorders improves at a rapid pace. Other advances were made, such as the development of promising new drugs for tuberculosis, cancer, HIV/AIDS, inflammatory diseases, and macular degeneration. There was the launch of a new and promising vaccine against increasingly dangerous staph infections and against the H5N1 avian flu virus.

What has this remarkable progress in medical research cost the American public over the past thirty years? The estimated total cumulative investment in the NIH per American over the thirty years is about $44 per American per year over the entire period. The future, I hope, will include sustained and substantial funding of biomedical research to both improve the health of the nation and to contain health-care costs.

As a physician, I am convinced that the only way we can truly meet the health challenges of the future is to move from the curative paradigm where we wait for disease to strike before we intervene to a more proactive stance where our science will allow us to identify a disease long before it strikes us and stop it in its tracks. This new era of medicine will be predictive, personalized, preemptive, and participatory. Let me describe some recent progress and let you imagine where it could lead in the next four to five decades.

1. *Preemptive.* Scientists at NIH recently developed and tested the first vaccine capable of protecting children from ages two to five against typhoid fever. The effectiveness of the vaccine—91.5 percent—is the highest reported for any typhoid vaccine. This is the first vaccine to protect young children. It is virtually free of the side effects that have been associated with other typhoid vaccines. This fever, if untreated, is debilitating and life-threatening. Typhoid is common in developing countries lacking adequate sewage and sanitation facilities. About 16 million people worldwide develop typhoid each year and more than a half million die from it. And this disease returns to our shores—four hundred cases occur in the United States each year; almost three quarters of those are acquired by Americans traveling abroad. In the global environment, the work we do to improve the state of the world improves our health as well. An even more telling example is the recent introduction of a cervical cancer vaccine which will, hopefully, eliminate this dreadful disease that strikes over 400,000 women worldwide each year.

By understanding that a virus, HPV, is the main trigger of this cancer, scientists were able to develop this revolutionary vaccine.

Many other teams of scientists are now working on other preemptive strategies including, for example, a possible vaccine for Alzheimer's disease.

2. *Predictive.* We know, from our NIH-supported research, that many of the most prevalent diseases of our time begin silently, many years before they inflict their obvious damage to patients. That will affect our grandchildren as they reach middle age, unless we act now. Increasingly, we are able to identify "biomarkers." Biomarkers are predictive of the likelihood of developing a disease or condition. Just in this past year, we have discovered genetic variations that help predict the development of age-related macular degeneration, a major cause of late-life blindness. We also discovered a new gene associated with Alzheimer's disease, a major control gene for diabetes, and a marker for prostate cancer risk. We have just begun to mine the power of the genetic resources we have developed to predict disease and intervene before the first symptom appears.

3. *Personalized.* Knowing who needs a treatment or who will not benefit; knowing what dosage will work for one patient and not for another; knowing, as we have discovered recently, that a newly developed test helps to determine the risk of recurrence for women who were treated for early-stage, estrogen-dependent breast cancer: this information can help a woman and her doctor decide whether or not she should receive chemotherapy, in addition to standard hormonal therapy. The test is one of many to emerge across diseases, to become available in the next half century. This particular test now being readied for FDA review and being evaluated in a long-term National Cancer Institute clinical trial has the potential to change medical practice by identifying tens of thousands of women each year who are unlikely to benefit from chemotherapy, sparing them from unnecessary and costly treatments and their harmful effects. In 2050, this individualized application of medical knowledge will improve outcomes for individuals. There will not be a "one size fits all" treatment, but a precisely tailored approach for each patient based on accurate diagnostic tests of the specific molecules and genetic subtypes we know now exist for each one of us and predictably derive the way we will respond to therapy.

4. *Participatory.* In 2050, we will see a public involved in promoting their own health, participating in research, and becoming health literate as part of personal and community education. Right now, according to new National Adult Literacy Study (NALS), more than half the US population struggles with basic information. Health literacy was measured by questions for the first time on that survey. Health literacy is the "degree to which individuals have the ability to obtain, process, and understand basic health information and services for appropriate health decisions." I particularly like that last part as it allows the public to understand and participate in their care and in decision making. When the Institute of Medicine embraced this initiative, they described health literacy as "where the expectations, preferences and skills of individuals seeking health information meet the expectations, preferences and skills of individuals providing the information." The level of educational participation by each individual will be key to the future, because most patients of the future

will not be sick as they will be treated preemptively. The Educational Testing Service (ETS) announced that the US literacy in the workplace has "eroded" and will continue to for at least the next quarter century. My hope is that we will recognize the threat this poses to the health of the nation, both in human and in fiscal terms. We tend to forget, as Einstein and Infield noted in 1938, "most of the fundamental ideas of science are essentially simple, and may, as a rule, be expressed in a language comprehensible to everyone." We must raise up our population, help them understand, and implement that understanding to improve human health.

We plan to see a future with less health disparity. ETS notes the Hispanic and African American graduation rates that peaked in 1969 and college attendance for these two groups that has been "stagnant" for the last ten years are "a perfect storm [that] continues to gain strength with no end in sight." We need these students to stay in school, learn, and those who are interested, to enter into science, or at least be interested in their health and the health of their families. And we need to understand the preemption, personalization, and prediction of diseases that are overrepresented in minority populations. All of us will experience an era of "online" medicine, when our vital health data will be fully electronic and continuously monitored at home to prevent irreversible damage to our health.

So, for the next half century, we must build upon a strong scaffolding of the discoveries we have made recently in genomics, proteomics, nanotechnology, and biomarkers that support new ideas, new investigators, seasoned mentors, and are fully inclusive. We will see those advances in basic, clinical, and translational settings. We will transform medical research and medicine to one that is focused on novel preemptive, predictive, personalized, and participatory strategies.

We need to free up the American genius for adapting itself to this challenge. The answers are not magic answers; they are the answers we receive from hard work. Only then will we see a healthy nation, unburdened by disease and the cost of disease, having an impact on the health and well-being of the entire planet. This will require also a complete and painful reform of our health-care system. Anything else is unthinkable.

36

Nancy G. Brinker

Nancy G. Brinker is founder of Susan G. Komen for the Cure, the world's largest grassroots network of breast cancer survivors and activists. She has served on the president's Cancer Panel and as US Ambassador to the Republic of Hungary and currently serves as Chief of Protocol at the US Department of State.

A World without Breast Cancer

What will the world look like in 2058?

Hopefully, we will at long last have realized our dream of a cure—or cures—for cancer, including breast cancer, so that no one ever again dies from this devastating disease.

Why "cures" instead of a single cure? Because cancer, including breast cancer, is not a single disease but many different diseases with different causes, presenting different risks for different people—women and men—and, therefore, requiring different treatments.

Ideally, by 2058 the "cure" will mean that researchers will have discovered how to prevent breast cancer in the first place. By then, if not sooner, a more complete understanding of the causes, growth, and spread of breast cancer—including the sequence of biological events that causes a cell to start turning cancerous—would mean that no one would ever again have to hear those terrible words: "You have breast cancer."

We already know, for example, that women with one of the so-called "breast cancer genes"—BRCA1 or BRCA2—have a much higher chance of developing the disease in their lifetimes. Although mutations of these genes currently account for only a small percentage of breast cancer cases, we're constantly learning more about the human genome—our genetic blueprint—and how different genes interact and mutate into diseases.

Looking ahead, it's possible to imagine a day when women are offered simple genetic tests—perhaps blood or saliva tests—to better predict which women are at greatest risk, followed by a variety of targeted treatments that actually prevent their genes from turning cancerous in the first place. In fact, we may even have a breast cancer vaccine, or different vaccines for the different kinds of breast cancer women develop.

As we learn more about the non-inherited factors that increase a person's risk of breast cancer—such as aging, being overweight or not exercising, having dense breasts, or having children later in life or not at all—women will be empowered with more effective ways to reduce their risk. Combined with healthy lifestyles, the treatments of tomorrow—like today's tamoxifen, which has been shown to help reduce the risk of breast cancer recurrence in some high-risk women—could help women greatly reduce their chances of developing breast cancer.

Short of prevention, the "cure" could also mean that breast cancer becomes a manageable condition. While some already speak of breast cancer becoming a chronic disease—not unlike diabetes, which can be managed but not cured—we have even higher hopes. We can imagine a day when breast cancer is no longer life-threatening and when treatments are akin to those for strep throat or a fractured finger—easily treatable, without terrible side effects, and from which the patient fully recovers.

In this scenario, breast cancer would be identified at its earliest stages when treatments are most effective and the patient has the highest chance of survival. Already, the five-year survival rate for breast cancer—before it spreads beyond the breast—is 98 percent. In contrast, the survival rate for metastatic breast cancer—when the disease spreads beyond the breast—is 26 percent.

Today, in 2008, technologies like mammography—and for some women, magnetic resonance imaging—are becoming more effective at detecting smaller and smaller tumors. For women with an especially aggressive form of the disease (HER2-positive breast cancer), the drug Herceptin is reducing the chance of a recurrence and increasing the chance of survival. A new generation of personalized medicine offers hope of tailoring treatments to the unique circumstances of individual patients. Nanotechnologies the size of atoms could transform cancer treatment by infiltrating and destroying cancer cells without the horrible side effects—and collateral damage to surrounding healthy tissue and organs—of some of today's chemotherapy and radiation.

Nanotechnologies the size of atoms could transform cancer treatment by infiltrating and destroying cancer cells without the horrible side effects.

It's possible to imagine a woman being told, "You have breast cancer, but because we detected it so early and because treatments are so effective and painless, you won't even know you had it."

Of course, it's one thing to imagine a world without breast cancer, or cancer in general. It's quite another thing to realize it. So how do we get from the world we have today to the world we want tomorrow?

First, we must recognize cancer as the grave crisis it is. Every year more Americans die from the disease (about 550,000) than died in all the wars of the twentieth century combined. If terrorists unleashed a biological attack on US soil that started killing 1,500 Americans every day—as cancer does—wouldn't we mobilize every national resource, public and private, to find an antidote or cure?

This is a crisis of access. Behind headlines heralding the potential of new cancer drugs lies the reality that thousands of patients struggle to pay as much as $50,000 for a course of treatment. Meanwhile, a cruel combination of poverty, racial disparities, and dysfunctional health policies means that many Americans—racial and ethnic minorities, the poor, those with little or no insurance—are less likely to receive quality cancer care and are therefore more likely to die. We cannot even begin to urgently confront the cancer crisis until we acknowledge these painful realities.

Second, we need a renewed national commitment equal to this crisis. The federal government spends roughly $5 billion annually researching cancer, a disease that costs our nation more than $200 billion every year in medical costs and lost productivity. Moreover, when inflation is factored in, funding for the National Institutes of Health—though at a record high by historical standards—has remained essentially flat for several years.

Ultimately, however, this is not a matter of money. It's a matter of will. The United States is the wealthiest nation in the history of mankind. We have the resources to wage a real war on cancer—if we want to. The cancer community—scientists, researchers, physicians, and patient advocates alike—can continue to help by forging consensus around a few priority research areas.

Third, a real war on cancer must liberate scientists and researchers from a scientific enterprise where funding shortfalls force investigators to spend increasing amounts of their valuable time searching for grants instead of searching for new treatments and cures. In addition, we must tear down the maze of cultural, clinical, and legal barriers that discourage the collaboration and revolutionary thinking necessary for high-risk, high-reward projects and major breakthroughs that will save lives.

For example, imagine the lives that could be saved if patients and researchers had greater access to the vast quanitites of human tissue and tumor specimens that hold the raw genetic material critical to research but that now sit unused on the shelves of laboratories, clinics, and hospitals. A more effective system for collecting, preserving, and tracking this tissue and specimens could help more patients qualify for the latest treatments and unleash a new era of genomic research and medical advances.

Finally, even as we face the challenges of today, we must prepare for tomorrow. Aging baby boomers are expected to cause a sharp increase in cancer diagnoses; a study published last year by the *Journal of Oncology Practice* predicted a 55 percent increase in the number of cancer patients by 2020, resulting in a dangerous shortage of cancer specialists and explosive health-care costs.

Globally, at least 7 million people die of cancer each year and nearly 11 million new cases are diagnosed—more than AIDS, tuberculosis, and malaria combined, according to Peter Boyle, director of the International Agency for Research on Cancer. In the West Bank, I met a Palestinian physician who spoke for many when he expressed fears of being overwhelmed by the coming "cancer tsunami."

Faced with this crisis, we cannot allow ourselves to retreat in despair. On the contrary, our hope and faith in a future we cannot yet see is our greatest strength. Over the past twenty-five years, millions of breast cancer patients and advocates, working and advocating from the grassroots to the highest levels of government, successfully changed the culture—how we talk about and treat this disease. And we can do it again.

After all, just consider the progress we've made in the *past* fifty years. Five decades ago, women with breast cancer lived in the shadows, afraid to even say the words "breast cancer" out loud. With mammograms still decades into the future, women who happened to find lumps in their breasts were often wheeled into an operating room for "one stage biopsies"—only to awaken with one or both of their breasts already removed. Generations of women—including my Aunt Rose—endured the painful and horribly disfiguring radical Halsted mastectomy, which removed the entire breast and underlying chest muscles.

In their wildest dreams, women like my Aunt Rose—and my sister, Susan G. Komen, who was diagnosed with breast cancer in the late 1970s and died in 1980—could never have imagined the treatments and survival rates we see today.

With the will to confront this disease as the global crisis it is, we can achieve our vision fifty years from today, and hopefully much sooner: a world without breast cancer.

37

Stanley B. Prusiner

Dr. Stanley B. Prusiner, a neurologist at the University of California, San Francisco, was awarded the Nobel Prize in Medicine in 1997 for his groundbreaking discovery of a new class of disease-causing agents called prions.

HOPE FOR PEOPLE WITH BRAIN DISEASES

Within fifty years, I am hopeful that biomedical scientists will be able to develop cures for degenerative brain diseases. If we are unsuccessful in our quest, the suffering caused by Alzheimer's, Parkinson's, and Creutzfeldt-Jakob diseases, as well as ALS (Lou Gehrig's disease), will grow to epidemic proportions. Why? Because the incidence of neurodegenerative diseases rises with age, and these illnesses will become more and more common as the life span of our population increases. If cures are not found, these brain diseases will constitute an enormous health problem in developed countries where people over the age of sixty-five are the fastest growing population group.

Alzheimer's disease, a much more widespread disorder than the other three neurodegenerative diseases, is already troublingly common. A recent study shows about five million cases of Alzheimer's in the United States today. Only approximately 200,000 of these cases occur among people aged 64 and younger. That number jumps to 300,000 in the sixty-five to seventy-four age group, and to 2.4 million in the 75–84 age group. Among Americans aged 85 or older, 2.2 million have Alzheimer's.

Stated slightly differently, 2 percent of Americans aged 65–74 now have Alzheimer's. This incidence climbs to about 20 percent in the 75–84 age group, and then jumps to a whopping 42 percent among Americans aged 85 and over.

Without cures, the problem of brain degeneration will only worsen as the population of our planet ages. This is not a uniquely American problem. Fast-forward fifty years, and let's take a look at China. There, the population over eighty years of age will likely increase from 12 million to 100 million people, according to United Nations statistics. Alzheimer's disease in that age group will jump from four million today to about 35 million. Numbers that large can seem meaningless, but 35 million is not much less than the 37 million people now inhabiting California. Imagine 95 percent of all Californians with a dementing illness. There is no escaping the fact that this is a *lot* of people!

The cost of such a widespread, debilitating disease is staggering. And it is not limited to victims of the disease. In the United States today, the loss of productivity, both among the victims of Alzheimer's and among their care-givers, adds up to an overwhelming $150 billion a year, according to the National Institutes of Health. Alzheimer's alone—excluding the three other less frequent neurodegenerative diseases—will bankrupt the US economy if we don't find a cure for it.

It does not appear that we are close to finding cures for neurodegenerative illnesses. In fact, the last major breakthrough in this area was the 1967 development of L-dopa for the treatment of Parkinson's disease.

But while we are still not close to cures for any of these four degenerative brain diseases, we have come a long way in understanding the nature of these illnesses. We now know that these four and several other neurodegenerative diseases are united by a common thread—the misprocessing of proteins. But the protein that is misprocessed is a different one in each of the diseases.

And even though we have learned a great deal about the relationship between protein misprocessing and degenerative brain disease, we do not know why Alzheimer's is five times more common than Parkinson's disease, why

Parkinson's is much more common than ALS, and why there is a much higher incidence of ALS than of Creutzfeldt-Jakob disease.

So how do we find cures for the neurodegenerative illnesses that cause so much suffering in so many people? One thing that is clear is that there will be no single wonder drug that can effectively fight all four illnesses. Since a different protein is misprocessed in each of the neurodegenerative diseases, a different drug must be found for each.

Scientists are hard at work to develop protein-specific drugs for each of the degenerative brain diseases. Researchers are looking primarily at two approaches. One is to block the misprocessing of the specific protein, or to prevent its aberrant behavior. The other approach is to get rid of the misprocessed protein, or to remove it from the brain.

Some scientists hope that stem cells will prove to be the secret to curing neurodegenerative illness. But stem cell treatment appears much more doable for other kinds of illnesses such as diabetes than for degenerative brain diseases. Currently, we do not know how to stimulate stem cells to make the proper connections or synapses after injection into the brain. And it is unlikely that we are close to knowing how to instruct these cells once they become neurons. We shall need to learn how to instruct the precise connections that will reestablish the functions that were impaired by the degeneration of the original neurons due to the accumulation of misprocessed proteins. Can we learn how to regenerate the damaged human brain by populating it with stem cells over the next fifty years? The answer is: we cannot predict! Scientists are sometimes great at making discoveries, but they are poor prognosticators of future breakthroughs. The most profound discoveries are neither predictable nor obvious even to the most learned scholars.

A key to treating neurodegenerative illness will be early detection. This is important because by the time symptoms are evident, the brain has suffered widespread degeneration. So to be most effective, a drug needs to be administered before symptoms are visible. This means making wide use of diagnostic procedures among seemingly healthy older people.

Fortunately, we have made great strides in the diagnosis of neurological diseases over the past three decades, and some of these advances can be applied to the neurodegenerative illnesses. Imaging technologies that include MRI and PET may prove helpful in the early detection of brain degeneration. PET imaging, in particular, offers many possibilities for targeting the specific proteins that are involved in each of the neurodegenerative illnesses.

As a scientist who has spent many years working to develop cures for the neurodegenerative diseases, I fervently hope that the picture fifty years from now will not be one in which tens of millions of people are suffering from Alzheimer's and other neurodegenerative diseases. As I grow older each year, my hope increases that the degenerative brain diseases will be eradicated soon, thanks to the creation of protein-specific drugs for each of these disorders.

38

Victor Sidel

*Victor Sidel, a physician and professor of social medicine at
Montefiore Medical Center, was co-founder and co-president of
International Physicians for the Prevention of Nuclear War (IPPNW),
the organization that received the Nobel Peace Prize in 1985. A former
president of the American Public Health Association, he is co-editor with
Dr. Barry Levy of* War and Public Health, Terrorism and Public Health,
and Social Injustice and Public Health, *all published by Oxford
University Press.*

A Physician's View of the Future

Looking fifty years forward when one has experienced more than fifty years in
the other direction requires an admission that widely divergent paths are
possible, dependent on the decisions we make not even five years hence, but
right now.

Since much of my professional life has been focused on two issues, it is
these I should like to consider: (1) providing medical care of excellent quality
equitably to all people and (2) preventing war, especially nuclear war, and promoting a culture of peace.

Medical Care Everywhere for Everyone

While I would be the last to decry the spectacular advances that have been made, and I believe will continue to be made, in the research that underlies medical practice, as well as in the technology we use to provide medical care, the people of our world in fifty years will be healthier only if we manage to redefine how we care for patients and, even more important, to ensure the social and environmental conditions in which health is protected and promoted. Too few of our practitioners today understand that no matter how skilled they may be, how personable in dealing with patients, how able to diagnose and prescribe, they are good physicians only when they are culturally competent and help enhance the conditions in which their patients live.

In the next fifty years, it is safe to assume that many practitioners in the United States will treat patients whose language and cultural heritage they do not share. The effective delivery of medical care requires sensitivity to this cultural gap. Medical care personnel who are not culturally sensitive cannot provide the care all their patients need. One way to deal with this problem is training many more practitioners who share language and ethnic identity with their patients. Another is training all practitioners in cultural competence and sensitivity.

We must remember, too, that cultural diversity properly harnessed is a force for better research. My wife and I were members of the first US medical delegation to visit China after the "Ping-Pong" breakthrough in 1971. (We were actually there at the same time that Henry Kissinger was working with officials in Beijing to prepare for then-President Nixon's 1972 visit.) There was great hope at that time for an exchange of knowledge that would mean we could learn about and use the practices, and particularly the goals for providing equitable care, that the Chinese advocated, and that they could in turn have access to and learn to use our advanced medical technology.

For the United States, the greater acceptance of nontraditional—or perhaps better said, multi-traditional—approaches holds enormous potential. If minds, laboratories, boundaries, and policymaking bodies remain open to change and focused on opportunity, the next fifty years may usher in a whole new dimension of care. Even more important, the United States will have to find ways to provide equitable medical care to all its people by making radical changes in the organization and funding of medical care.

In sum, in the twenty-first century we again are likely to see the greatest changes in the health of the peoples of the world deriving from social change, no matter how the technology changes. It can be argued that this is quite similar to what we witnessed in the nineteenth and twentieth centuries, when improved sanitation, safe drinking water, widespread immunization, and other changes in the conditions in which people live had far more significant health effects than changes in medical care.

We again are likely to see the greatest changes in the health of the peoples of the world deriving from social change, no matter how the technology changes.

In the United States, we particularly suffer from a persistent tendency to focus on the dramatic, when day-to-day problems deserve our attention. Five years ago we began to divert enormous attention and funding to defenses against bioterrorism, a potential threat, perhaps, but not a current reality. At that same time, there was insufficient attention to chronic disease and disability and to broader public health problems. Again, the choices are ours.

One War or One World

Nearly fifty years ago, 1961 to be exact, colleagues and I became part of a group of physicians in Boston dedicated to exploring and explaining the medical consequences of the use of nuclear weapons. This was the genesis of an organization, Physicians for Social Responsibility, which in 1980 became the US affiliate of the newly formed International Physicians for the Prevention of Nuclear War (IPPNW). Five years later, IPPNW was awarded the 1985

Nobel Peace Prize for its work on reducing the risk of nuclear war between the United States and the Soviet Union.

From the beginning our purpose was clear. As physicians we knew there was no way to deal with the health effects of nuclear war, having witnessed what had happened in Japan and then multiplied its impact one thousandfold in anticipation of the use of hydrogen bombs. The only choice was prevention of the use of nuclear weapons and their abolition.

In the decades since then, our work has continued and broadened, and our concern has increased. The choices made by United States political leaders today threaten to bring losses of incredible dimensions to our country, and perhaps within fifty years the loss of the country as we know it. The unwise and illegal attack on Iraq and the disastrous conduct of that war, with little concern for civilian and military casualties and for world opinion, could well drive a stake into the very heart of our ability to coexist with the peoples of the world, not to mention collaborate with them for the greater good of all concerned.

And the effect on people in the United States will very soon become even more evident. Advances in battlefield medicine, principally based on improvements in transportation that connect the wounded with appropriate care more quickly, have saved countless lives. But these injuries—both physical and mental—among the survivors are more extensive than those our society has seen in the past. We are in no way prepared to deal with them in ways that will allow for continued care and for successful assimilation of these men and women into our communities.

Even for those of us who have stayed at home, our near future will continue to be affected detrimentally for years to come because of the massive reductions in public funding that have been caused by war expenses and the simultaneous tax cuts our current administration instituted. The memorable phrase of John Kenneth Galbraith applies even more than before: ours is a nation characterized by "private affluence and public squalor."

Meanwhile, to deal with the causes of global warming that these same leaders can't quite admit we're facing, the United States is promoting the development of nuclear power before we have developed either the ability to deal effectively with the nuclear waste provided or to prevent the use of these power plants from producing fissile materials for nuclear weapons development.

Sad to say, the next fifty years may be bereft of the very decisions and developments that can produce a decent world order. At the very time we have developed the transportation, the technology, and the communication to become a global community, we are making choices that will cause disparities in income and wealth to increase. Unless we make fundamental changes, we are likely to be part of a world divided, if indeed we have a livable world at all. Sharing our enormous wealth, strengthening the international institutions we have weakened, and understanding our dependence on the other people of the world may yet save us and our planet, but only if we act now.

39

Claude Mandil

Claude Mandil is executive director of the International Energy Agency.
He is the former chairman and CEO of the Institut Français du Pétrole
(The French Oil Institute) and has held many high-level positions in the
French government and in the energy and research sectors.

CLEAN ENERGY FOR PROGRESS

I am an optimist. Fifty years from now the world will be a much nicer place. Five decades of scientific, technical, and economic progress, and the continuing growth of international trade, will have created a much more prosperous world than we have today. The global economy will have grown to four times its present size and the economies of developing countries more than six times. Energy will have a big role.

This will mean increased life expectancy and an opening up of opportunities for many. More people will have things that almost everyone values—pleasant and comfortable homes, decent sanitation and water, freedom to travel, high-quality education and health care, modern appliances, and access to a wide range of leisure activities. Living standards will increase for almost everyone. But the most dramatic changes will have been in places such as India and China, Latin America, and Africa, where growth will have been most rapid and where, for the first time in recent history, a majority of ordinary people will have a real share in economic progress.

We are going to need a lot of energy to drive these changes. Energy for buildings and infrastructure; energy for industry and transport; energy for heating and cooling, and for appliances. We are going to have to meet a global demand for energy services that will be at least three times greater than today.

Yet carbon emissions from today's energy supply already represent a grave threat to our environment, and we face increasing tensions in oil, and to some extent, also gas markets. How will this huge increase in energy needs be met without making these problems much worse? It's our job, in the International Energy Agency, to advise governments on this question.

The answer is that, by 2050, a fundamental transformation will need to have taken place.[1] We will need a much cleaner and more efficient energy economy than we have today.

The old incandescent light bulb—which produced mainly heat and not very much light—will be a relic. So will many of today's inefficient electric appliances.

In my optimistic future, there will have been a far reaching change in attitudes to energy supply and use. I don't mean by this that people will be constantly worried about their energy consumption or trying to cut back or economize. Probably most people will not be particularly aware of the change, from day to day, because it will have become a part of the culture. But when the people of 2050 look back to our own generation, the change will be evident. They will be astonished at the needless waste and pollution that was tolerated. The old incandescent light bulb—which produced mainly heat and not very much light—will be a relic. So will many of today's inefficient electric appliances—especially those that use almost as much energy on "standby" as they do in full operation. The fact that houses, offices, and shops were designed and built with little regard to efficiency, thereby requiring about ten times as much energy as necessary to heat and cool, will seem extraordinary. And I think there will be shock and perhaps revulsion that the atmosphere was once treated as a free dump for the millions of tons of CO_2 that power stations, factories, buildings, and vehicles emit every day.

Houses and other buildings will be much better insulated in 2050 with carefully planned ventilation to reduce energy needs. The differences will not be obvious to the occupants, except on their electricity and gas bills! "Heat pumps" drawing on the naturally stable temperature of the earth will maintain comfortable temperatures drawing on minimal amounts of electric power. Solar energy collectors will be built into the structures of new buildings, and small local wind and hydrogenerators will be common.

"Heat pumps" drawing on the naturally stable temperature of the earth will maintain comfortable temperatures drawing on minimal amounts of electric power.

It will be an electric age, drawing on electric power that is clean, silent, and flexible in use. I don't know what exciting new appliances will have been invented by 2050. Perhaps we will all have robots in our homes? But I expect they will be powered by electricity.

By 2050, we will have many more clean ways of generation. Smaller and more advanced nuclear reactors, with fail-safe designs and generating the absolute minimum of nuclear waste, will be common in many countries. And renewable generators, capturing the energy of the sun, the oceans, and the deep earth, will proliferate. Coal is abundant in some of the countries, such as China and India, which will see the fastest economic growth. A lot of coal will still be used in power stations. But new materials and much higher steam temperatures will have increased their efficiency. And the CO_2 emissions will be captured and stored safely in naturally occurring underground reservoirs of salt water—not vented into the atmosphere. Other pollutants, such as sulphur and nitrogen, will be removed at the same time. And perhaps some technologies we don't even have in mind will be on the drawing boards.

More advanced and flexible electric grids will balance the use of local and renewable energy sources against the larger centralized power stations that will continue to provide backup and bulk energy.

Heavy industry has been making great strides, all over the world, in reducing energy costs. It makes business sense. By 2050, not only will business processes be much more efficient, but waste, heat, and materials, as well as industrial products, will be comprehensively recycled. And the biggest industrial users of fossil fuels (oil, gas, and coal), like the power stations, will be storing their CO_2 emissions underground.

What about transport? Cities will be designed for convenience, with offices, shops, and leisure facilities close to residential areas and with well-developed public transport. Fewer people will be forced to start each day by getting into a car.

It's hard to predict when the long reign of gasoline and the internal combustion engine will come to an end. It has many decades to run yet, and there is still plenty of potential for further improvements in efficiency. However, eventually, there are two low-carbon technologies that could provide alternatives: "cellulosic" biofuels—converted from straw and other vegetable wastes— and electric vehicles powered either by batteries or hydrogen fuel cells. They need a lot more development and, in some cases, technical breakthroughs, before they can achieve the necessary performance, reliability, and cost. Most probably we will see some combination of these technologies. Electric vehicles will mean cities with clean air and much less noise. And they will be fun to drive because the power range of an electric motor is much wider than that of an internal combustion engine. You don't need so many gears and you can have lively performance!

Underpinning all this will be advances in basic science to bring forward new technologies and reduce the costs of those that we have. For instance, nanotechnology may give us lighter and tougher materials; we may have cheaper chemicals to convert sunlight into electric power; superconductivity may give us more efficient electric grids; and biotechnology may reduce the costs and environmental impact of biofuels.

With the changes that I have described, we can accommodate the increase in global demand for energy services whilst decreasing global CO_2 emissions. Coal, oil, and gas still meet most of the world's energy needs in 2050, but we will use them in a more intelligent way. In particular, the growth of the world's oil demand will be moderated. As a result, we will have well-functioning and stable global oil markets, benefiting both producers and consumers.

It's an attractive picture. It isn't going to be easy to reach this "brave new world" of energy that I have described. The transition is going to demand a great effort. But once we have achieved a cleaner and more efficient global energy economy, the benefits will be apparent to everyone.

In this optimistic future, change will have been brought about because governments in all parts of the world, businesses, and consumers will have realized in the first decade of the twenty-first century that change was both essential and urgent. And they will have decided to launch an unprecedented global effort in the face of a shared threat.

As a result, agreement will have been reached on a set of international treaties committing each nation to making its fair contribution to reducing CO_2 emissions. This framework will have included strong economic incentives for low-carbon energy options, probably including a global market in "credits" awarded for CO_2 savings. It will have been a triumph of diplomacy and will be one of the key pillars for peace and security in the world.

Governments will also have taken far-reaching steps to accelerate low carbon and efficient technologies. These will have included the promotion of research and development, demonstration, and deployment, as well as regulation and public information. Governments in the developed world will have taken the lead in helping to make the best technologies available in the developing world. The costs of such programs are not beyond reach. But a substantial switch of resources into the energy sector will have been required.

Farsighted business leaders will have pioneered the new technologies, often in partnership with government. Taking advantage of the new incentives, they will have made the investments needed to develop new energy infrastructure and bring new products to the mass market. Energy-aware consumers will have decided to buy the efficient appliances and houses that become available, to recycle their waste, and to use public transport when convenient. And some will be generating their own clean energy.

That's my optimistic picture of what the world could be like in 2050. Of course, it is not the only future that is possible. Another possible future is "business as usual," in which, despite a certain amount of rhetoric and good intentions, we take no decisive action to change the energy outlook. In that case, I am afraid, the future is bleak and, indeed, hot. Global CO_2 emissions could be more than double today's level leading, according to the latest international expert assessment (IPCC), to global temperature increases of 5–6°C. Oil demand would be more than 90 percent higher than today, increasing the risk of tensions in oil markets and leading to growing pressure of international competition for access to scarce energy resources. That's the pathway that we're on at the moment. It would probably collapse in a crisis well before fifty years.

The decision is ours to make. It is urgent, because energy infrastructure is built up over many years and will take a long time to change. Viewed in this light, even 2050 isn't very far away. Let's make the right decisions now so that, in our children's generation, the optimists turn out to be right!

40

Nancy Ho

Nancy Ho is a leading scientist in ethanol energy research. She received the R&D 100 Award for genetically modifying yeast to convert sugar into fuel. She is a research molecular biologist and group leader of the Molecular Genetics Group at the Laboratory of Renewable Resources Engineering at Purdue University.

CO_2 FOR GOOD

When I was a little girl, growing up in rural China, I dreamed that I could see and talk to any person that I happened to think about. That was more than sixty years ago, and I had never seen a telephone. As a child, I was not considered a prodigy in science or even a clever little girl. In fact, just the opposite; most people I grew up with considered me dumb and unremarkable because I was sick much of my childhood. Fortunately, what I lacked in physical strength, I more than made up for with imagination. Nevertheless, this dream has been fulfilled. Nowadays, we can see and talk to a person by simply dialing a number and turning on a screen.

Human desire is very powerful. Constructive desire will lead to progress. In the past fifty years, there must have been quite a few people with ingenious minds besides that unremarkable little girl in rural China. They all shared that same desire and made things happen.

More than twenty-five years ago, I was given the opportunity to develop recombinant baker's yeast to enable it to convert the unusual sugar known as xylose to ethanol. Xylose is present in large amounts in polymers of plant matter collectively known as cellulosic biomass. At the time, there were nearly ten groups throughout the world attempting to accomplish this task. After five years of painstaking research by scientists worldwide, no approaches were successful. As such, the scientific community believed that it might not be possible to achieve this goal.

I had the strong desire to enable baker's yeast to have this capability. Mankind has relied on this safe, friendly little microbe to make bread and produce wine for thousands of years throughout the world. This yeast is also used in industry to produce millions of gallons of ethanol from crops such as corn. My wish had been to see the same safe microbe used for the production of ethanol from cellulosic biomass, a much more abundantly available feedstock to help provide the world's need for transportation fuel. Twenty years ago, driven by my faith in science and my desire to contribute to society, my coworkers and I found a way to overcome the crucial obstacles to make yeast ferment xylose to ethanol. Our work made it possible for scientists all over the world to continue working on the project and to perfect the development of the recombinant yeast to co-ferment glucose and xylose to ethanol. As a result, the genetically engineered yeast has now been used in the early stages of industrial ethanol production from crop residues such as wheat straw, corn stalk, and switchgrass.

I believe the day for easily converting CO_2 into energy without solely relying on land or water to grow plants will happen within the next fifty years.

For the future, I have the desire to see yet another vast untapped resource used for energy. When we burn coal for electricity, produce ethanol from crops or cellulosic biomass, or drive our cars to and fro, we waste considerable energy as carbon dioxide that's released into the air. It is this carbon dioxide in the form of greenhouse gasses that has exceeded the capacity of the natural plant kingdom to absorb it, leading to climate change. I believe the day for easily converting CO_2 (carbon dioxide) into energy without solely relying on land or water to grow plants will happen within the next fifty years. I am confident that other scientists and engineers throughout the world also have a similar desire. Simple biological and physical methods will someday be developed to directly convert CO_2 to useful fuels. When that day comes, the energy stored in plants, coal, and petroleum will become fully utilized and recyclable, and the world will never be short of energy. Thus, I advise those who hold the reserves of coal and petroleum not to waste your treasure unnecessarily, but to save them for the day when technology enables us to safely and easily exploit them.

41

Michael Shermer

Dr. Michael Shermer is executive director of the Skeptics Society and the author of Why Darwin Matters: Evolution and the Case Against Intelligent Design *and* How We Believe: Science, Skepticism, and the Search for God. *He is the founding publisher of* Skeptic *magazine and a monthly columnist for* Scientific American.

TO OPEN THE WORLD TO ALL PEOPLE

For many years I have been involved in a Seattle-based organization called Foundation for the Future, created by the aerospace entrepreneur and philanthropist Walter Kistler, in which a group of scientists and scholars from various fields meet once a year to discuss what life will be like in the year 3000, among other lofty topics. It is a delightfully stimulating way to spend a weekend, but I do not for a moment think that any of us has any idea of what we are talking about when we talk about life a thousand years from now. If most experts on the Soviet Union in the mid-1980s had no idea that the empire would collapse by the end of the decade, and if most computer scientists in the early 1980s were largely clueless to the forthcoming rise of the World Wide Web within a decade, how on earth can anyone possibly fathom what changes will be wrought a hundred decades from now?

The problem with envisioning long-term economic and political change is that we have been entrenched in political states with top-down directed economies for so many millennia that it is nigh impossible to imagine how human relations could peacefully prosper in any social system other than the one to which we have grown accustomed. By the logic of the *status-quo bias*, nature has endowed us to hold dear what is ours and leads us to opt for whatever it is we are used to having. Still, history's long clock and evolution's deep time afford us the opportunity to pull back and see the bigger picture of where we might be headed in the next half century.

As a species, fully modern humans are roughly one hundred thousand years old. For the first ninety thousand years, everyone everywhere on the planet lived in small bands of hunter-gatherers, organized in egalitarian economies and simple political systems. Then, at the end of the last Ice Age, roughly thirteen thousand years ago, population numbers in numerous places around the globe exploded in size. Hunting and gathering did not produce enough calories to support these larger populations, which led inexorably to farming and the Neolithic Revolution. The domestication of large mammals and edible grains generated the necessary calories to support ever-increasing populations, which led to additional physical and social technologies that facilitated even larger populations, and so on, in a positive feedback loop.

How and when different peoples made the transition from small bands and tribes to large chiefdoms and states was determined, in part, by the carrying capacity of the environment and the population size of the groups that, in turn, determined the social structure of societies and the forms of exchange, trade, and coexistence with other groups. After living for ninety thousand years in one lifestyle, humans shifted from hunting and gathering to agriculture in the course of just a few thousand years in a number of places around the globe. The evidence indicates that the transition was largely driven by environmental economics: as populations grew larger, the hunting-gathering lifestyle was incapable of supplying sufficient calories, which led to the development of more effective means of food production.

The concomitant leap in food production and population was accompanied by a shift from bands and tribes to chiefdoms and states, and the development of appropriate social organizations and technologies. People began to live in semipermanent and then permanent settlements, which led to land ownership and private property, and surplus foods, tools, and other products that formed the basis of nascent trading economies. This led naturally to the development of a division of labor in both economic and social spheres. Full-time artisans, craftsmen, and scribes worked within a social structure organized and run by full-time politicians, statesmen, and bureaucrats. Organized religion came of age to fill many roles, not the least of which was the justification of power for the ruling elite. The intertwining of politics and religion has been found in nearly every chiefdom and state society around the world, including the Middle East, Near East, Far East, North and South America, and the Polynesian Pacific islands, in which the chief, pharaoh, king, queen, monarch, emperor, sovereign, or ruler of whatever title claimed a relationship to God or the gods, who purportedly benighted them with the power to act on behalf of the deity. States developed into bona fide civilizations, cults evolved into world religions, and barter markets emerged into full-fledged economies.

With the rise of chiefdoms, states, and empires, it was no longer possible to separate politics from economics. Although the natural condition of hunter-gatherer bands and tribes is one of egalitarianism, the equal redistribution of economic wealth has never been realized in larger societies. As well, without the proper social institutions to enable and enforce fair and free exchange between groups, violence and war often erupts. An explanation comes from evolutionary economics. One of the prime triggers of between-group violence is competition for scarce resources. There are rarely enough means to support all individuals in all groups. Once that capacity is exceeded, the demand for those resources will exceed the supply. Such was the condition throughout most of history for most peoples in most places. The formula is straightforward: population abundance plus resource scarcity equals conflict. Thus, one way to attenuate between-group violence is to increase the supply of resources to meet the demands of those in need of them.

The psychology behind defusing intergroup aggression involves the process of turning potentially dangerous total strangers into prospectively helpful honorary friends. This is enabled through the creation of social institutions that encourage, enable, and enforce positive social interactions that lead to trust. One of the most powerful of these forms of interactions is trade, the effects of which I want to elevate into a principle based on an observation by the nineteenth-century French economist Frédéric Bastiat: "Where goods do not cross frontiers, armies will."

Bastiat's Principle not only helps us understand how hunter-gatherers made the transition to consumer traders, it also illuminates one of the primary causes of conflict; its corollary elucidates one of the principal steps toward conflict reduction. If Bastiat's Principle holds that *where goods do not cross frontiers, armies will*, then its corollary dictates that *where goods do cross frontiers, armies will not*. This is a principle, not a law, since there are exceptions both historically and today. Trade will not prevent war, but it does minimize its likelihood. Thinking in terms of probabilities instead of absolutes, trade between groups increases the probability that peaceful and stable relations will continue and decreases the probability that instabilities and conflicts will erupt.

Although free trade is not a surefire prophylactic for between-group conflict, it is an integral component to establishing trust between strangers that lessens the potential volatility that naturally exists whenever groups come into contact with one another, especially over the allocation of scarce resources. As well, since I believe that market capitalism and liberal democracy are tightly linked, I should note that there is a well-documented correlation between liberal democracy and peace—the more a nation embraces liberal democracy the less likely it is to go to war, especially against another liberal democracy. One study, for example, found that of the 371 international wars that occurred between 1816 and 2005 in which at least one thousand people were killed, there were 205 wars between nondemocratic nations, 166 wars between democratic and nondemocratic nations, and 0 wars between democratic nations.

Conclusion: *Power kills, democracy saves*. Solution: *spread democracy*. Likewise with Bastiat's Principle. Conclusion: *Trade leads to peace and prosperity*. Solution: *Spread trade*. Will liberal democracy and market capitalism spread throughout the world in the next fifty years? If we draw a trend line from, say, 250 years ago to the present, that line shooting out for the next fifty years would seem to point to an affirmative answer. So I am optimistic, despite the dismal setbacks in the Middle East, Africa, North Korea, and other parts of the world where totalitarianism and religious fundamentalism rule, but as Thomas Jefferson said: "The price of freedom is eternal vigilance."

Given our dual disposition to be both good and evil, and the power of the environment to elicit one or the other, we must *choose* freedom, then create the circumstances in which it can be realized, and then defend it once it is achieved. So freedom begins with an idea, and a conscious choice to attain it. Can the mere raising of people's consciousness work to trigger social change that leads to an increase in freedom? Of course it can. If it couldn't there would have been no civil rights movement, we'd still be practicing slavery, and women could not vote. How do we get from here to there? The slow but steady spread of liberal democracy and market capitalism, the establishment of environments that spawn interpersonal and international trust, the transparency of political power and economic hegemony, the availability and accessibility of all knowledge for everyone everywhere, and the opening up of political and economic borders that will serve, in the words on a plaque posted at the Suez Canal:

Aperire Terram Gentibus
To Open the World to All People

42

Joseph L. Bryant

Joseph L. Bryant, DVM, is director of the Animal Model Division of the
Institute of Human Virology at the University of Maryland School of
Medicine. As a researcher, his primary responsibility is developing animal
models for studying the pathogenesis of AIDS and cancers.

The View as I Glide By

As I glide down the street in my new hydroelectric booster shoes, several school children fly by me in the new calibrated helium-efficient high draft propulsion-in-flight shoes. These new high-draft propulsion shoes send them speeding past me at speeds of more than 10 mph. They are elevated some two feet from the pavement. I am sure they like the idea of soaring around the town with these shoes propelling them as though they were in flight, because if I were younger maybe I would enjoy the shoes too. They are perhaps too cumbersome for someone as old as I am. Although I am aged, I never thought I would live to be over a hundred years old and on my way to work. The hydroelectric booster shoes are just fine for me, and they send me along the road with the smooth gliding force that doesn't jar me or cause me to stumble.

The cars are also elevated as they move through the traffic with the anti-crash sensors surrounding them. They fly at an elevation of three to four feet above the road. They are smaller and seat four people comfortably. The most important feature of these cars is the fact that the government has finally approved a fuel for cars that does not damage the ozone layer. And these cars hover above the ground with space shuttle precision-guided panels that are programmed to search out one's destination before leaving home. However, there are fewer cars on the road now, because most people enjoy getting their exercise by walking with their hydroelectric booster or jet-propelled shoes rather than being ferried along in a car.

The cars are also elevated as they move through the traffic with the anti-crash sensors surrounding them.

I pull out my personal assistant from my coat pocket, which looks like a radio or Palm Pilot from fifty years ago. I start the day by dictating a letter to the company's headquarters about the personnel management team. My personal assistant allows me time to think and time to work while I'm on my way to the office. My note is as follows: "as a researcher and veterinarian who specializes in animals, I must profess that science and technology have come a long way in eradicating diseases in the world. With the technology that we have today, most diseases of the past are gone, but a new threat lurks in the minds of all mankind. That threat is the culmination of people being obsessed with power and wanting to control not only their lands but the whole world and the people."

Years ago I used animals in my research to help me to learn about different medicines and new technologies to help eradicate diseases such as cancers, AIDS, and bacteria-resistant bugs. Now the new threats to mankind are man-made diseases that are biologically engineered in a world that had conquered nuclear threats. Nuclear proliferation has come to a halt. Each day a new and more deadly engineered biological threat faces mankind. My job is to develop mice and rats with a DNA structure that will allow scientists to quickly maneuver our "Whole Body Evolutionary Beam," which can be programmed to deliver an essential amount of medication to the body of anyone who is sick.

The "Whole Body Evolutionary Beam" was developed about thirty years ago in a laboratory in North Carolina. The idea of the beam was to capture as much atmospheric electromagnetic and ultraviolet light as possible and to send a charge through a person's body and heal it of any ailment known to mankind. However, man can be cruel to his brother. We can find cures for everything but the callous lack of respect and hatred that man has always been plagued with from the start of time.

Biological and environmental wars are raging everywhere.

Biological and environmental wars are raging everywhere. Man has become a maniacal monster when it comes to controlling and having power over people. So as the days wear on, we are faced with the burden of solving new and more powerful synthetic diseases that arise often in a society that is rich in personal possessions, but lacks a heart of gold.

43

Barry Marshall

Barry Marshall, senior principal research fellow in the School of Biomedical, Biomolecular & Chemical Sciences at the University of Western Australia, shared the Nobel Prize in Medicine in 2005 with Robin Warren for their discovery of the bacterium Helicobacter pylori *and its role in gastritis and peptic ulcer disease.*

ONE TUESDAY IN AUSTRALIA

Fifty years from now.

In the next fifty years, many of the technologies invented during the twentieth century will bear fruit so that we will use them, probably unconsciously, in our daily lives. The goal of these advances will be to give us longer, more interesting lives, with less uncertainty about the future. In addition, as these advances are miniaturized and become far less expensive and generic, they will be available to everyone, even people in the poorest countries.

So let us imagine the average working day in Australia, say a Tuesday morning in April. I used Tuesday because work time will be less and all weekends will be long weekends, with Monday off. Monday was always a difficult day in any case, and people are far more likely to be unwell on Mondays as evidenced by statistics for all kinds of "sickies," as sudden days off are called.

So Tuesday morning at 7 a.m. I wake up, quite easily, because the temperature of the bedroom has gradually increased over the past hour from cooler night mode to warmer day mode, and the lighting has been increasing to daylight brightness during that time. Actually, in April the days are still long so the curtains open, allowing natural sunrise to come in the room. I stand up and stagger into the bathroom, watching my urine stream pass over the medical diagnostic monitor on the side of the toilet. The morning news, playing on the flat screen on the wall above the bowl, shrinks in size as the lower half of the screen is replaced by a graph. Hmm, cholesterol up slightly today, blood sugar okay, vitamin levels in the normal range, antibody titres a bit low; must remember to take some vaccine probiotics this week. I say okay, and the recommended health-care items are added to the shopping list.

"Thank goodness we have solved the global warming issues, and those crazy water restrictions have ended."

I have a quick shower, brush my teeth, and shave, then stand for a few seconds while air blowers dry me off. I finish the job with a small toweling square the size of a handkerchief as I say to myself, "Thank goodness we have solved the global warming issues, and those crazy water restrictions have ended." I recall the sales brochure of the bathroom reprocessor showing the shower water passing through the heat exchanger, being osmotically cleaned and then sterilized before reentering the 50°C storage tank. I reflect upon the amount of stainless steel being used in everything these days, and the price of my nickel shares. I wander around the house, coffee in hand, watching the morning news. As I pass in front of a window, it automatically "smokes up" in case I haven't dressed yet—which I haven't.

After dressing, I decide to work at home today, as 75 percent of people can do these days. I don my virtual reality headset and visit my virtual office, discuss the day's activities with my secretary, take a stroll around the laboratory office, and then accompany my research staff for a quick ward round. After chatting with the patients, I make recommendations for treatment, and the new medications are delivered in a few minutes, by internal robotic courier to the patients' bedsides.

These days very few medical problems turn up "out of the blue," as they used to. We all know our own genomes inside out, and have the choice of taking measures that protect or prevent most of the diseases that used to be called "hereditary." And with most people working from home, the yearly cycles of colds and flu have long ago disappeared in developed countries. In any case, the vaccines these days are continuously upgraded and added to the food supply, so viruses are having a very hard time of it.

By midday the work is done, so my wife, Adrienne, and I decide to take a walk up to the shops and then do some gardening. The main purpose of this is to get some exercise, and a two-mile stroll outside seems far more healthy than a boring treadmill. It is about 75 degrees in the neighborhood, sunny and breezy. After an hour we return home, unpack the groceries, and take a nap for forty minutes. Then Adrienne digs in the garden, installing two new plant species that have just been developed—randomly colored tulips which apparently flower all winter. Again, it is all good exercise, which is the one thing becoming harder to do these days. While digging, she chats to one of our children in the United States who has experience with this plant variety. I amuse myself, driving a tiny video robot down one of the garden ant-holes. I have a lot of respect for the not-so-humble Aussie garden ant. After they released the restrictions on GMO life-forms, it only took a few years for the designer ants to completely annihilate the pesticide business, at least in my garden. Grasshoppers here will rue the day they landed near any of these little mothers!

Advances in biology have certainly solved most of the problems we used to experience with outdoor living in Perth, Western Australia. In developing countries, the high-priced luxury plants and "garden guard" ants we city slickers depend on are less used, but more important technologies have spun off as a result. Even in Africa, crop failures, plagues, and pests are rare events now that the nutritionally enhanced cereals and customized insect pest controls have

I look forward to the prospect of eating a couple of hot dogs with ketchup, as I do at every game. At least some things never change.

been implemented. Globalization, no longer a controversial issue, has resulted in political stability and many new markets for African products. Maybe we should take a holiday there next year. It would be nice to visit the Gorilla park in Rwanda, but I have heard we would need to book early. We might also visit the Gates Malaria Museum, and try to make the whole trip a tax deduction.

My watch beeps and reminds me that it is time to catch the Virgin shuttle for the game at the Barry Bonds Stadium. I look forward to the prospect of eating a couple of hot dogs with ketchup, as I do at every game. At least some things never change. I might choose to take the moving sidewalk tonight; my 106 years are starting to tell.

44

Carl Pope, Daniel Becker, and Allison Forbes

Carl Pope is executive director of the Sierra Club, America's oldest, largest, and most influential grassroots environmental organization. Daniel Becker and Allison Forbes are director and conservation organizer, respectively, of Sierra Club's Global Warming Program.

WAKE-UP CALL ON GLOBAL WARMING

You wake up to a clear day. Out the window, sun hits the solar array and reflects off wind turbines generating electricity on a distant hillside. Your home heat and light monitoring system begins to wake up, too, engaging a transparent liquid crystal filament in the windows to block heat when the sunlight pours in, avoiding the need for more air conditioning. Your personal organizer gauges your mood before selecting a music stream and presenting the news of the day. Video messages include a request from your boss that you use your full virtual office to tour the new concentrating solar power plant with her that afternoon lest you miss any details.

Since the unprecedented warming of the earth's atmosphere over the last century, life on Earth has become necessarily deliberate, efficient, and, well, clean. In the twenty-first century, we have learned to live within our carbon means.

Five decades ago, mankind's greatest environmental, ecological, and economic challenge loomed large: traditional methods of energy production based on the extraction and combustion of oil and coal led to massive shifts in the climate's equilibrium. The rate of warming caused by an atmosphere charged with carbon dioxide and other heat-trapping greenhouse gases threatened communities across the planet. Fortunately, we rose to the climate challenge.

The ingenuity of America's engineers produced a revolution in clean vehicles and renewable energy captured from the sun, wind, and waves.

The ingenuity of America's engineers produced a revolution in clean vehicles and renewable energy captured from the sun, wind, and waves. The United States made money and created new jobs by exporting clean energy and storage technologies to China and India, allowing them to develop into sustainable modern economies. Just as cell phones allowed these nations to "leapfrog" over the installation of landline telephones, renewable technologies enabled them to avoid years of dependence on dirty coal and oil.

Engineers have also changed the way people travel. Hover technologies are based on the use of magnetic levitation, which increased the efficiency of Japanese and European trains in the late twentieth century. In the twenty-first, they revolutionized the US transportation system. Energy savings made mass transit affordable to build and cheap to run.

A comprehensive network of maglev "rails" has made private ownership of cars redundant and allowed governments to replace paved superhighways with solar collectors and carbon-absorbing trees and grasses that can be turned into a biofuel. A commuter can now request a transit lift from his or her pocket organizer. The request is correlated with hundreds of others in the region and new routes activated every five minutes.

Constant adjustments by the smart planning system make rail travel extremely efficient. To maximize nonstop traffic flow, generally, rails elevated twenty to thirty feet off the ground travel east and west, while those raised ten to twenty feet travel north and south. Local lines and access ramps are at ground level. Even clean school buses run on the rail system. Since buses and cars no longer idle beside the schoolyard, spewing toxic exhaust near the playground, the rates of childhood asthma and respiratory illnesses have plummeted.

Community development plans that integrate home, business, and commercial spaces have further reduced commutes. Most office workers telecommute from home or walk several blocks to a neighborhood satellite telecommuting office building where they can link to coworkers in real time. Here they enjoy all the benefits of a central office and workplace interactions without the burden of lengthy, energy-consumptive travel.

In the United States, energy production has diversified away from a twentieth-century portfolio of oil, nuclear, and coal. In North Dakota, cows graze and farmers harvest fields beneath tall wind turbines. Solar harvesting is centered in Florida, Nevada, Arizona, and New Mexico. But most of the nation's rooftops, many sidewalks, and bike paths sport solar-collecting tiles and pavements that power the neighborhood and feed excess energy into the regional grid. Advanced battery storage systems save up for rainy days. Coastal states harness energy from waves and tides. Superconducting cable and updated microwaves transfer surplus energy to cities. Of course, there were up-front costs, but the savings are huge.

As efficiency measures boost consumer energy savings, people have more money to spend on America's new clean technology products. In 2020, the United Steelworkers Union pioneered the new industry of disassembly, providing recycled parts to manufacturers and sometimes reassembling unique vehicles, homes, and entertainment systems. The union taught America that it was more efficient, and therefore cheaper, to reuse discarded parts than to produce new ones. For example, the federal government was able to build modern low-income housing units from the recycled bodies of gas-guzzling automobiles.

Even as we reduce emissions, we continue to feel the effects of an atmosphere we had overloaded with carbon. Early international investment in efficiency, wind, and solar energy helped us avoid the worst potential threats of global warming. We could not, however, avoid the rising sea levels. Monsoons that flooded Bangladesh in 2004, covering 24 percent of the nation in polluted water, did not prepare the country for the tragic losses of the last twenty years. Levee construction has cost Gulf Coast states billions of dollars but has created thousands of new jobs. Nonetheless, Florida is still fighting the Atlantic Ocean's efforts to subdivide the state into an archipelago.

Warmer winters helped tropical varieties of mosquitoes spread across the nation, carrying Dengue fever and other diseases. Storms and severe weather patterns have increased, wildlife habitats have shifted, and glaciers have shrunk and disappeared. But, as carbon emissions begin to level off, humanity is learning to take its first big breath of relief.

At night, parents take their children outside to locate the "energy stars" amid a thick blanket of twinkling lights in the sky. Above the interference from our atmosphere, these satellites collect the sun's rays and beam energy back to earth.

Of course, we could have woken up in 2050 to a different reality.

Smog obscures the distant hillside. Lights, computer, and music power up automatically with energy produced by coal and nuclear power plants. A car waits in the driveway, but the highway to work is congested and smog-choked. The weather display reports a typical heat wave and smog alert for this afternoon, and a digital note reminds you to pick up new asthma inhalers for the kids.

• • •

"I think we have a very brief window of opportunity to deal with climate change . . . no longer than a decade, at the most."

—James Hansen,
Director, NASA's Goddard Institute
for Space Studies 2006.

45

Keith B. Richburg

Keith B. Richburg is a longtime reporter and foreign correspondent for the Washington Post, *serving as Bureau Chief in Manila, Nairobi, Hong Kong, and Paris. During his nineteen years abroad for the* Post, *he covered the war in Afghanistan and the invasion of Iraq, the start of the 2001 Palestinian intifada, the 1997 Hong Kong handover to China, the 1992 US intervention in Somalia, and the 1994 genocide in Rwanda. He is the author of* Out of America: A Black Man Confronts Africa *and a member of the Council on Foreign Relations.*

DATELINE: 50 YEARS INTO THE FUTURE

I count myself as an optimist.

The latter half of the twenty-first century will be a period of expanded prosperity for the planet. Advances in medical science will have prolonged human life. Cancer and Alzheimer's disease will be treatable conditions, and a new, universally-available vaccine against AIDS (whose French and American inventors will have jointly shared the Nobel Prize) will have led to a global baby boom. The soaring worldwide birthrate will have erased all earlier worries about an aging, graying population of retirees without the workforce to sustain it. With people living healthier, and longer, the working life will have also been expanded by more than a decade.

The world will be mostly urbanized—nearly three-quarters of humans living in some one hundred "megacities," led by the Chinese metropolises of Shanghai, Tianjin, and central Chongqing, which long ago surpassed Detroit as the world's automaking capital. But a new environmental awareness that took hold early in the century has meant a development largely free of harmful emissions destroying the atmosphere. The earth will be a cleaner place.

The expanded prosperity will mean fewer wars. The majority of the ten billion or so people on the planet will live in democracies, with guaranteed freedoms and more universal respect for human rights. Borders will in many places seem like anachronistic relics of an earlier generation; the United States of Africa will, by 2050, have followed the European Union and the East Asian Union in facilitating the flow of people, goods, and ideas freely across vast areas.

The world will be a more multiracial place, much like Brazil is today.

Instant communications through cyberspace and high-speed air travel will make the world truly "flat." With the movement of people will come the mixing of people; racial and ethnic "categories" will become increasingly meaningless. The world will be a more multiracial place, much like Brazil is today. The global economy will be interconnected, as old rivalries give way to a shared planetary prosperity. The economies of China, India, Brazil, Indonesia, and Nigeria will be the world's largest; Brazil, Indonesia, Nigeria, and Mexico will have followed Germany and Japan as the newest members of the UN Security Council.

New technologies in rice production will allow the world to feed itself. New rice seed varieties, invented at the Philippine labs of the International Rice Research Institute, will be able to grow in drought conditions, in flood, or in the craggy hard earth of some places now considered desolate and inhospitable.

Chinese will have joined English and Spanish as the world's most globally used languages.

There will be problems, to be sure. A few nativists in some isolated corners will continue to decry the free movement of people and the spread of a global "race" as an erosion of traditional and distinct ethnicities and cultures. Some languages spoken only by a shrinking few—think Northern Europe—will be in serious danger of disappearing from the planet without concerted efforts to save them. Danish and Swedish and Dutch will risk going the way of Welsh and Gaelic.

Entertainment at the mid-century mark will have reached a level of true inter-activity; from the multidimensional console, the viewer can virtually transplant himself to the scenes of his favorite films, taking the roles of different characters and watching how the scripts change and the other actors interact with his or her presence. I, for one, plan to take on the role of Rick in *Casablanca,* and share a romance in Paris with Ilsa Lund on the eve of the German invasion before moving to Morocco to open Richburg's Café Americain.

And fifty years from today, *Casablanca* will still be considered the best film of all time, one hundred fifteen years after it first opened in cinemas.

46

Gregory A. Poland

Gregory A. Poland is professor of medicine, infectious diseases, and molecular pharmacology and experimental therapeutics at the Mayo Clinic College of Medicine, and director of the Mayo Vaccine Research Group and the Program in Translational Immunovirology and Biodefense.

LEAPS AND EUREKAS

Among the most satisfying and anticipated advances in the future will occur in the world of medicine. The best and most intelligent guess is just that—a guess. But both recent history and a keen awareness of the current directions in science and medicine can inform a reasonable look forward as to the future of medicine. However, two caveats are in order: 1) The hallmark of science and medicine has been unanticipated great "leaps" forward—the "eureka" moments, if you will, and 2) such progress only occurs to the extent the public is willing to provide the crucial funds for research that allow such discoveries.

Among the big leaps forward will be major advances in the prevention of disease; biologic-based treatments of mental illnesses; increasingly noninvasive methods of imaging, diagnosis, and treatment; and the institutionalization of individualized medicine.

Prevention of disease will become the major focus of medical care, rather than the current focus on disease and its treatment. Vaccines against diseases that we find are the result of chronic infections will be developed, and vaccines against cancer will become commonplace. Vaccines against diseases currently not thought of as vaccine-preventable will become so—diseases like atherosclerotic heart disease, diabetes, dental caries, autoimmune diseases such as lupus and rheumatoid arthritis, obesity, and multiple sclerosis. These miracles will advance on the wave of deeper insights into the immune system and our ability to suppress, activate, and manipulate it at will. In addition, vaccination to prevent pregnancy is highly likely. Many of these vaccines will convert currently deadly illnesses and diseases such as cancer into minor issues—much as vaccines against measles and smallpox have virtually eliminated these diseases from the lexicon of fear known to modern man.

Vaccines against cancer will become commonplace.

New "prophylactic" drugs or supplements will be developed to prevent further progression of physiologic processes toward disease. Such drugs will be safe, effective, taken only periodically, and inexpensive. Different methods of drug administration such as nasal sprays, skin patches, eye drops, and depot injections lasting months will be developed. It is possible that such drugs will prevent obesity, diabetes, arthritis, depression, and other illnesses before they occur.

Important advances in the treatment of mental illnesses will occur as we increasingly understand the biologic basis of psychiatric diseases and begin to abandon centuries-old concepts of experiences and family upbringing as exclusively causative of illness. In part, we will begin to understand certain human "hardwiring" characteristics as "at risk" under certain conditions for producing disease. Already the biologic basis of depression has been elucidated, and increasingly drugs will be discovered and precisely targeted to treat these disorders. Preventive psychiatry, whereby mental illness can be prevented before it becomes floridly manifest, will have its ascendancy and result in a healthier, happier society. In time, some of these diseases will become as easy to treat as once-lethal diseases that are routinely treated today, such as thyroid disorders and diabetes.

New, noninvasive methods of imaging will become commonplace and their use vastly accelerated in the areas of diagnosis, screening, and treatment. Diseases now requiring major invasive surgical procedures will be handled as routine office procedures, many performed by robotic instrumentation incapable of error and capable of exceedingly fine movements detectable only under great magnification. For example, laser treatment of coronary artery plaques that cause angina will be treated at first by threading a small catheter into a leg artery up into the coronary circulation and then vaporized. In time, such treatments could occur by injecting microscopic spheres coated with a tracer activated to release a burst of laser or other type of energy field when it reaches the area of narrowing. Treatment will take minutes, and the patient will get up and immediately resume usual activity.

Imaging to look for tumors, areas of infection, or other abnormalities will occur at a microscopic level of resolution and allow physicians to see and diagnose illnesses at such an early stage previously unattainable. The advent of imaging modalities such as PET scanning will encourage additional development of imaging modalities that will allow us to visualize physiologic processes occurring in real time. For example, we will begin to recognize abnormal functioning predictive of disease onset very early when prophylactic treatments can prevent progression to frank disease and disorder. In turn, life span will increase. Over the last one hundred years, the life span in the United States has almost doubled. Further increases are likely as we learn to prevent disease at the earliest stages

Among the biggest challenges will be lifestyles and behaviors associated with affluence— obesity, stress, and lack of exercise in a leisure-loving society.

possible. However, among the biggest challenges will be lifestyles and behaviors associated with affluence—obesity, stress, and lack of exercise in a leisure-loving society. The physical exam of the mid- to late twenty-first century will be characterized by a full-body, in-depth scan taking minutes and a drop of blood for genetic and abnormal function testing.

Finally, a major advance will be the establishment of individualized medicine into standard medical practice. The concept of individualized medicine is to allow physicians to treat patients on a truly individual, precise, and specific basis, recognizing that there is a genetic, immunologic, and physiologic spectrum extending from "normal" to "abnormal." In turn, this results in differences in how we metabolize drugs, whether we are likely to have minor or serious side effects to those drugs, and whether we will respond to them in a therapeutic manner that treats the disease target. In fact, work is already in place that will allow physicians to test the state of tens of thousands of genes or enzyme activities simultaneously with a single drop of blood on a "gene chip." This is already in practice for single genes or disorders, but further advances will allow an assessment of the entire genome of an individual. The results of these assays will allow physicians to precisely target the right therapy, to the right patient, at the right time, and achieve the right result, at a fraction of today's costs associated with empiric "trial and error" treatment that characterizes current medical practice.

47

Earl G. Brown

Earl G. Brown, a specialist in influenza virus evolution, is a virologist in the Department of Biochemistry, Microbiology and Immunology Faculty of Medicine at the University of Ottawa.

SNAPSHOTS OF THE FUTURE WITH INFECTIOUS DISEASE: LIVING IN A BRAVE NEW WORLD WITH AGE-OLD SCOURGES

Through the Looking-glass Darkly

We all know that predicting the future is precarious, and this is only accentuated when considering the future of infectious disease, because the principal characters causing these diseases, microbes, are changeable. You have to know where you've been and how you got there in order to know where you are going. Although our scientific understanding is improving, the intricacies and drivers of infectious disease are only partially appreciated. Looking through this glass tells us that microbes change rapidly in response to a changing environment, and that the trend to increased crowding of humans with animals is increasing the genesis of damaging pathogens.

The Future, How Did We Get There from Here?

There is a quip going around infectious disease circles that the nineteenth century was followed by the twentieth century that was followed by the dark ages. The point being, we are losing our battles with infectious diseases. How can this be happening in a time of such scientific progress? In general, infectious diseases are evolving at breakneck speeds and undermining our control measures. Because vaccines and drugs work through binding of compounds to microbial surfaces, natural selection acts on microbes to change their shape and become more slippery. Alternatively, they may weaken our grasp by attacking our gripping abilities. The microbes are quick-change artists, and in this changing world they reign supreme. In a world of vaccines and antimicrobial drugs, microbes must become resistant to these therapies. So the future will bring more of the same old arms race—but we will make better and smarter bullets and the "bugs" will keep blocking and interfering with our expanding armamentarium. This is a perilous game that we won't change until it is obvious that we have to, and that time may be nearing.

In the future we will attempt to mold and change the environment so that we do not select resistant and dangerous microorganisms. Because the majority of novel human infections come from animals, we must focus on the environmental factors affecting interactions of human and animal populations. One of the constant drivers of microbial evolution to high virulence is population density. The two factors that drive rapid evolution are a changed environment (i.e., a new drug or vaccine) and people in close contact. This is exacerbated by the global trend of urbanization, especially in Asia where each megalopolis is surrounded by factory farms that feed the citizens. Intensive animal production facilities produce the cheapest meat, but, unfortunately, these meat factories are also "disease factories," a concept elaborated by Paul Ewald, a pioneer in the field of evolution of infectious disease. For example, the highly pathogenic avian H5N1 influenza virus was generated in factory farms in Southeast Asia.

Whether you have produced a disease factory may not be entirely obvious.

This is the case in modern hospitals that are supposed to be "disease-treatment factories"; however, the rate of hospital-acquired infections is burgeoning. An individual now has a 15 percent chance of acquiring an infection during a stay in a hospital. Although hospitals are the best places for treatment, they are generating the nastiest infections, because people with the worst infection bring the worst bugs to the hospital, where they become entrenched. So a cycle is established that must be broken. Highly virulent and drug-resistant microorganisms are continuously becoming established in our hospitals, popularizing names like VRE, MRSA and *C. difficile*. Worse, the spread of these nasty agents into the community now threatens everyone.

Where Have We Been, and How Did We Get Here?

Fears of pestilence are well-grounded in history, as human populations have been ravaged and laid low, time and time again, by epidemics. In some of the darker times, such as plague-ridden Europe in the 1600s, life span was curtailed to an average twenty-four years. Fortunately, major technological advancements in the last two hundred years have stretched average life expectancies dramatically; most notably, the germ theory of disease leading to improved hygiene, and more recent advancements in vaccines and the development of antibiotics.

This spurred the surgeon general to declare victory in the war on infectious diseases in 1967. This was overly optimistic as the current state of affairs has seen the repeated emergence of new diseases and the reemergence of old ones. But things seemed rosy in 1967 thanks to recent technological advances, especially those in the new field of virology that had accelerated research and development of drugs and vaccines. The scourge of small pox, an annual killer of multimillions, was on the verge of eradication through vaccination. The epidemics of flaccid paralysis due to poliovirus in the '50s that killed and maimed many became a thing of the past with the rapid development of not one, but two kinds of vaccines developed by Salk and Sabin. Vaccines were being made against most of the common human childhood diseases with the first mumps vaccine rolling out in 1967, preventing the second most common infectious cause of deafness. Parents sighed with relief, and people eagerly rolled up their sleeves to arm their immune systems against infections. In addition, medical science had generated many different classes and formulations of antibiotics to effectively treat most bacterial infections.

It appeared that infectious diseases were no longer a problem because we had "all" the solutions. So what went wrong? Why are old infectious diseases returning with a vengeance, and why are we seeing all these new emerging ones?

Now a generation later our antibiotics and vaccines are failing. HIV has popped out of nature to infect sixty million, and other new pathogens (like SARS-CoV and toxigenic E. coli) show up at the rate of about one per year. The answer hinges on the rate of reproduction. Humans can only reproduce in thirty-year cycles, whereas microbes may reproduce every thirty minutes. Population size matters, and microbial populations of billions arise overnight. It is rare to encounter the one-in-a-billion resistance-conferring mutations among the sea of random mutations, yet when you have ten billion organisms you have ten mutations, each of which ups the ante in the ratcheting up of resistance or virulence.

The Future: Fighting Fire with Fire

On a more optimistic note, in fifty years we will be reaping the rewards of advanced scientific accomplishments where we harness the power of microorganisms to fight disease. We will cure cancers with therapeutic viruses and bacteria that specifically attack tumors. Using other microbial therapeutics, friendly microbes will be pitted against disease-causing ones in order to protect us against infection. So we will fight AIDS with anti-HIV virus, a currently hypothetical virus that cannot grow in healthy cells but can only grow in HIV-infected cells to destroy them or alternatively block infection of the

> *We will cure cancers with therapeutic viruses and bacteria that specifically attack tumors.*

uninfected. We also will get immune system transplants or boosts given by injection to fight or prevent diseases, so instead of mounting an immune response to cure an infection, we will skip that step and get immunity immediately in a syringe shot. Vaccinology will have progressed to produce a vaccine against currently intractable foes such as HIV and hepatitis C virus.

Other vaccine treatments will control viruses and bacteria that cause obesity, Alzheimer's disease, autism, and many autoimmune diseases.

Following the recognition that most chronic diseases are caused by infections, we will vaccinate against heart disease and cancer. New infectious agents will be discovered, as well as the disease-causing properties of microbes, either alone or in combination, that we had not previously linked with diseases that occurred much later. Other vaccine treatments will control viruses and bacteria that cause obesity, Alzheimer's disease, autism, and many autoimmune diseases.

Major advancements will be made in predicting the disease-causing potential of microorganisms and the disease susceptibility of humans. This will come from our new ability to read the genomes (gene sets) of humans and microbes like a book. The story will be one of biological susceptibilities, capabilities, and histories. We will be able to predict who will be more likely to get infected and who will get serious complications.

Rapid point-of-care diagnosis will be routine.

Antibiotics and anti-infectives will be developed, including entirely novel types of antibiotics, and will also include gene-based therapies where bits of DNA or RNA (a fragile cousin with attack capabilities) are used to fight infectious agents.

You may ask why we continue to use these failure-prone, high-tech band-aid solutions. The answer is that these technologies save lives. And while prevention through environmental management is best, we will still need to treat life-threatening infections. The trick then is not to render them useless through abuse and overuse.

Playing with Fire and Getting Burned

Although we will have many new capabilities for fighting disease, we will also be facing more microbial threats. Accordingly, humanity will continue to face an aggressively changing microbial world where we will increasingly have new and more serious infectious diseases from the increased urbanization and high-density animal rearing. We will learn to pronounce the names dengue, chikungunya, and other now-exotic viruses as they become global pathogens. Hepatitis viruses are now letter A–E; we will use another five letters for new ones.

All first-generation vaccines will have failed and we only will use "third-generation" vaccines and multidrug therapies to slow the acquisition of resistance in pathogens. Tuberculosis (TB) will return with a vengeance to the developed world in the form of highly virulent and drug-resistant variants such as extremely drug-resistant (XDR) TB that is now rearing its ugly head among AIDS patients in many countries.

Seasonal human influenza will become more aggressive (what goes around, comes around), and at least one novel influenza pandemic will occur before 2058, but the mortality rate will be moderate and will not significantly affect global population growth. Many new respiratory pathogens that cause atypical pneumonia similar to SARS will have arisen and produced short pandemics; we will number them consecutively, i.e., SARS-II–III, etc. Bioterrorists will be able to make pathogens that only damage people with particular types of genes, opening the way for making designer pathogens targeted to their enemies. This will still be tricky business and less effective as the world becomes one inter-mixed population. Sex will continue to be a risk as more sexually transmitted diseases arise, and other types of human contacts will be restricted; the handshake and other skin contact will be reserved for family members. Human populations will become more susceptible to serious infection as the number of people living with chronic diseases or suppressed immune systems from diseases (such as HIV) and transplant therapy continues to increase. Dedicated hospitals will treat infectious diseases, and there will be zero tolerance of hospital acquired infection. And just in case you were wondering, yes, this will be expensive, but cheaper than the alternatives imposed by spiraling hospital acquired infections. Unless great strides are made in animal diseases, meat eating will be weighed against the societal risks of disease generation and transmission. Mad cow disease and other related prion (infectious protein) diseases will have decimated wild and domestic animal herds and led to declining meat consumption. Nonanimal sources of meat will become popular, including germ-free techno and engineered meat. The trend will be to local small-scale sustainable agriculture.

The Future Present

We will continue to live simultaneously in the best and in some of the worst of times. The debate will center on how to break the increasing deadly arms race between microbes and humans. We will have come to the realization that with respect to infectious disease (to paraphrase the forty-first president), "It's the environment, stupid!" And from Walt Kelly's Pogo, "We have met the enemy and he is us," where we identify the problem and we work with it from its source. Since primordial times, all life on the planet has been coexisting with and shaped by interactions with microbes. We cannot extricate ourselves from microbes but must instead shape a symbiosis to mutually benefit our continued survival.

48

Carol Bellamy

Carol Bellamy served as the executive director of UNICEF and was the
first former volunteer to serve as director of the Peace Corps. She is
currently president and CEO of World Learning, an international non-
profit organization with operations in seventy-seven countries that fosters
global citizenship through experiential education and community-based
development work.

THE AGE OF THE GLOBAL CITIZEN

In my ten years at UNICEF I witnessed, again and again, the dire consequences
of failing to protect the most innocent and vulnerable. For me, it is always the
individual stories of deprivation and the faces of young victims that I remember most and where I locate both my outrage and my hope.

When I look at the gap between rich and poor nations, the exploitation of
children as sex slaves or child soldiers, or widespread war and genocide, I see
in those issues not the inevitability of suffering but a crisis of leadership and
a failure to make necessary choices. In my years of service with the United
Nations, I verified over and over again that poverty doesn't persist because of
nothing; war doesn't emerge from nowhere; HIV/AIDS doesn't spread in ways
we don't understand. These are our choices, and for the most part, we've not
chosen well. We need to shape a generation of compassionate new leaders who

will take the action needed and make the hard choices today's leaders have too often chosen to defer.

How might we do this? The answer may start with a very simple notion—sending young people abroad to learn about themselves, the world, and their place in it.

At World Learning, the organization I now lead, we send three thousand young ambassadors abroad each year to walk across differences and see the world through the eyes of others. When I meet the young leaders who emerge transformed from these and similar programs, with new skills and new capacities to understand and with a heartfelt desire to give back to those less fortunate, I am strongly encouraged and filled with hope for the future.

These young leaders include college students like Sara Franklin, who returned recently from our study abroad program in South Africa and wrote of her experience there: "I can say with absolute certainty that I have been permanently altered by what I have seen, the people I have met, and the reflections which have resulted from my time here. My belief that people must band together to fight for one another, that kindness and a commitment to prioritizing those in need, has come to color every conversation I have and every fleeting thought of what I may do with the rest of my life."

My vision for a new era of leadership—an era that might come to be called the "Age of the Global Citizen"—begins, modestly, with sending more young people like Sara abroad each year to connect across cultures and religions, share homes and meals, and realize our common humanity. In this vision, by 2058 every young person would make this journey, whether across continents, national borders, or ethnic divides. Success would be measured not in miles covered but in degrees of enlightenment achieved. It would become a global rite of passage.

The global citizens touched by these experiences will share a set of critical leadership qualities now in far too short supply:

- They will be more likely to see diversity as enriching, not threatening;
- They will understand the intimate connection between local acts and global impacts;

- They will feel compassion and responsibility for those outside their tribes, religions, political parties, and borders;

- They will be as tolerant of other views as they are intolerant of human suffering wherever it occurs; and

- They will excel at listening and be masters of understanding.

"In the Age of the Global Citizen," historians of the future will reflect, "leaders were less likely to look the other way in the face of injustice. They were more inclined to put a face on the faceless, and give voice to the voiceless. They did not hesitate to act boldly and compassionately when innocent lives were at stake."

This is the world as I'd like it to be in fifty years. This is a world I'd be proud to call home.

49

James Canton

*James Canton is CEO and chairman of the Institute for Global Futures
and author of* The Extreme Future: The Top Trends That Will Reshape
the World for the Next 5, 10 and 20 Years *and* Technofutures: How
Leading-Edge Innovations Will Transform Business in the 21st
Century. *Named "The Digital Guru" by CNN and "Dr. Future" by
Yahoo, he is an authority on future trends in innovation.*

Some Words from "Dr. Future"

As a futurist who advises organizations worldwide, my work is about better
preparing leaders and organizations about what is coming next—the risks
and opportunities. Often it is about just getting people to think about the
future as a long-term narrative of open possibilities whose outcomes they can
influence. My future horizon investigation is divided into multiyear phases:
short-term or one to three years; midterm or five to ten years; and long-term,
the time exceeding ten years. The insights I have learned also remind me that
the future is born of a convergence of trends—lifestyle, health, economics,
security, to name a few—not one domain. I have developed a holistic approach
to forecasting that has been useful.

Population is a case in point. In the decade between 2050 and 2060, how
many people there are and where they live will be of substantial concern. Let's

consider first the number: over nine billion people are expected to inhabit the earth at that point. We will need careful planning and adroit use of technology to bolster the carrying capacity of our planet and feed, clothe, and produce habitat for these people. Today, one-sixth of the people in the world have never seen a glass of clean water. We cannot afford to have three billion people in that category in the future. The big future trend question is will the carrying capacity of the earth be able to meet the needs of an explosive population? We must prepare for this future today.

And where will they live? There are likely to be two hundred to three hundred megacities, three out of four of them in coastal areas where the risk of floods, storms, etc., is most extreme in the future by 2040. At the same time, it is not unreasonable to expect a divide that might even be described as a chasm to develop between the aging developed economies—United States, Europe, Japan, and perhaps by then, China—where the birth rate is being contained by shared values and governmental policy, and the developing world—Africa, Latin America, and the other countries in Asia—characterized by a youth boom and developing middle class. Figure into that equation the fact that of the 1.3 billion people in China today, nearly one-half are under the age of twenty-five.

China's rise in economic and political power, already watched carefully by many, is only one element of a significant realignment of nation states. A new superpower is emerging that will set a new dynamic in play worldwide. I believe the intimate collaboration between the West and Asia must be a force for future security, stability, and progress for the entire planet. But there is much work to be undertaken to enable this to come to pass. We need to cross the cultural divide of suspicion and fear that threatens this vital future view.

One of the chief issues is poverty and war—they go together. Right now we live in a world where there are fifteen to twenty "micro-wars" going on at any given time. We simply cannot tolerate that level of conflict in fifty years. By then, demands for water and other natural resources will have escalated dramatically. Our current understanding of climate change should provide sufficient warning that for issues such as these there are no instant fixes. When you consider the risk of future wars given forecasts of extreme climate, poverty, and conflict over natural resources, you begin to realize that there are no quick fixes that will bring peace and security without immense change and cooperation among nations. The challenges that face humanity are daunting to say the least.

We need twenty to fifty years of planning and development, and a public that demands leaders who think both strategically and holistically. I would maintain that this is the real challenge that confronts us—the right courageous leaders who have bold visions for the future.

The global GDP today is 3 to 4 percent. In fifty years it *must* be 7 to 10 percent to keep pace with global population change. Innovation is the key driver for both the developed and developing worlds, and there are four specific building blocks: information technology, life sciences, nanotechnology (the redesign of matter at the atomic level), and neurotechnology. Advanced tech will create jobs, security, and progress for a world that is hungry for innovation. Innovation is the key driver of the global economy and, I might add, peace and security. Innovation goes hand in hand with democracy. The more nations that embrace democracy—free minds, free markets, free enterprise less war, poverty, and conflict. The conflict between innovation-based democracies and religious and secular fundamentalist dictatorships will define the future of the planet in the twenty-first century.

While it can be argued—and I do—that because of the innovation deriving from American industry, the United States must regain a position of leadership not just in security but in science, health, and education, it is equally true that decisions we make henceforth must be driven by concern for the well-being of the whole world. The Kyoto Protocol controversy, embroiled in the discussion of who gets to pollute and how much, is a prime example of wrong thinking. Right thinking says we are all in this together. Developed nations must help developing nations catch up. Giving them a pass on polluting is hardly the answer. Developing incentives whereby a cessation of pollution will produce access to innovation is the productive tack. In essence, we need a Marshall Plan for a global future.

We also fall prey to incomplete thinking on the health-care front—and the effects fifty years hence could be disastrous. There are those who insist the burgeoning cost of health care may well bankrupt government programs. The question is not whether we can afford health care. It is instead, how we can transform health care so that all are served?

We have known for more than thirty years that by changing lifestyles we will simultaneously save people and ease the burden on society. Yet we still have no really good incentives for individuals to manage their own health status. Whether the system be socialized medicine or managed care, the costs *will* go up. I fully expect that within not fifty but ten years, the entire system will need to change. Then we must:

- Agree that self-care is the critical missing piece, and devise education programs and incentives to radically increase individual responsibility. We shall each know our personal genome and be able to predict our future health.

- Optimize our potential for the use of new medical breakthroughs by communicating potential risk factors and focusing on technology that will not only treat but prevent illness.

- Be aware that we face a high risk of future pandemic based on the confluence of increased travel, rapidly growing population in areas where water and food sources are challenged and people are in close contact with birds and animals, and the consequent potential mutation (and therefore resistance to treatment) of different diseases.

- Recognize that global terrorism may at some point be carried out on the biological level, and search for a means to create a world where social stability and international understanding counter the impulse to maim and kill.

The record of humans taking care of each other must improve, and I am hopeful that it will. It is all too easy to predict the future and forget that we also can—and I believe must—shape it. We all can agree to take the risks necessary to shape outcomes in a way that will benefit humanity as a whole. Collaborative thinking and behavior have never been more important. We have the opportunity to create a future that is prosperous, productive, and peaceful. We need to better plan for and envision a future of our design, not one of chance. We need to have the courage to invent solutions with an eye to the future. We need to embrace innovation and democracy for all. I encourage all to meet the challenges of the future by better preparing today.

50

Douglas Osheroff

Douglas Osheroff, professor of physics and applied physics at Stanford University, shared the Nobel Prize in Physics in 1996 for discovery of superfluidity in helium-3.

SOME WARNINGS, SOME WORRIES, AND A CALL FOR LEADERSHIP

The future we face in fifty years, or in ten, will be significantly affected by our ability to deal with crises. There are several crises already at our doorstep and more we can see coming. Rather than arguing whether they are happening or will happen, our task is to focus on what we will do about them.

In terms of immediacy, I would point first to global warming. The situation is potentially (and maybe already) lethal. Although humanity as a whole right now is consuming more oil than it is finding, still very little effort is going into developing nonconventional forms of fossil fuels, not to mention alternative sources of energy. Continuing on this course will destabilize the world in many different ways, to wit:

- Right now we have enough coal that, should we use it with no limitation, we will totally foul our atmosphere.

- The Greenland ice cap, there for millions of years, is changing in measurable, frightening ways, and the very real possibility exists that it will totally melt away.

- We cannot predict what humanity will do if, in fact, the changes in climate cause large areas now being farmed to either dry up or end up under water. We can expect, however, that the short-term effects will be huge, and will lead to massive loss of life.

The ever increasing levels of CO_2 in our atmosphere are not the only reason we should curtail our burning of fossil fuels. Petroleum in particular is a valuable raw material for use in manufacturing. As we use up all natural deposits of ores from which we derive metals such as iron and aluminum, we must rely more and more heavily on plastics in construction, which are produced from petroleum.

A second issue that will shape the future, perhaps of less immediacy, but certainly of no less importance, is the issue of global understanding. Having for most of its history boasted about its "melting pot" status, the United States continues to embrace a cosmopolitan society. Many classes of jobs in our country are filled by foreign workers, both legally and illegally in this country. My colleagues and I working in the sciences are just as aware of the many Asians who work here in research laboratories, filling technological and engineering positions. Potential terrorism is not the only reason why cultural understanding is important. What's more, as national boundaries melt in the face of global markets, we need a reliable means of addressing how the survival of the planet can become as important as economic prosperity and creature comforts. It's easy to point the finger at China's use of coal, for example. It is more difficult to understand that much of that coal is used to produce goods that the world as a whole is consuming.

A third issue is that of population growth. The world's population, moving toward nine billion, is straining this planet's resources in terms of food and water, let alone any of the creature comforts we so desire. Yet the distribution of wealth is far from uniform, and it is well understood that people with less education and a poorer quality of life have the highest birthrates. We must embrace our responsibilities to share education, technology, and the potential for prosperity.

There are those who say that fifty years hence we will be on our way to providing a partial solution to the population issue by developing space travel. That is dangerous thinking. Ours is the most hospitable planet in the solar system. If we want to invest in the future of mankind, we'll need to do it here.

What is the future of transportation? This is an activity that is responsible for the consumption of much of the world's petroleum. Certainly we can gain a factor-of-two increase in efficiency for automobiles, but not without substantial changes in their size and shape. Air travel seems to be near the limits of what is possible, however, given economic and physical constraints. It is interesting to consider why the Concorde failed; not because it didn't do what it promised to do, but because ultimately it was not economically competitive. It also seems unlikely that the scram jet will produce a revolution in air travel, although it might lead to a cheaper means to orbit Earth. Excessive use of this complex and expensive technology would deposit nitric oxide very high in our atmosphere, however, further threatening the ozone layer. In short, the hopeful mantra one reads at the Epcot Center in Disney World—"If you can dream it, you can do it"—is becoming more and more difficult to accept.

The electronics and communications industries are still living off the advances of the twentieth century. Moore's Law is alive, but perhaps not well. We need new technologies that will do more, faster, and while generating less heat per clock cycle than ever before. The promise of optical fiber communications is real, but it continues to offer more than the consumer needs or is willing to support. Yet it seems clear that we can and should expect further revelations in computation and communications over the next fifty years.

Finally, while I would in no way describe myself as politically active, my concern for the future based on recent events in the United States has led me to become more vocal. Global warming obviously is compelling in and of itself, but the issues are legion: the failure of the United States to play a leadership role in our efforts to curtail greenhouse gas emissions, the war in Iraq and its spurious genesis, political and religious (but not scientific) objections to stem cell research, the broader apparent conflict between the religious right and science, all give me cause for concern. Adding to these the fact that our news media are being controlled by a smaller and smaller number of very wealthy and powerful people, and I have concern for the very political processes that support our democracy.

Finding a future we will all enjoy in fifty years requires choosing leaders who are informed, visionary, and conscientious. I hope we will.

51

Lyman Page

Lyman Page is a cosmologist and professor of physics at Princeton University, where he measures the spatial temperature variations in the cosmic microwave background, the thermal afterglow of the big bang.

How Our Knowledge Will Increase

Let me take a few moments to say where we are before guessing where we may be in fifty years. My particular branch of physics and astronomy is called cosmology. We study the large scale structure of the universe. In the past fifteen years we have pinned down the age of the universe to 13.7 billion years to within an uncertainty of 200 million years, roughly the time since the dinosaurs roamed the earth. We now know that the universe is made of just 4 percent of the stuff of which we are made, 22 percent of some new type of matter never seen on Earth, and 74 percent of some new kind of force or energy that has yet to find explanation in any fundamental theory of Nature. We know a lot about the universe, but there are clearly major questions that may take fifty years to answer.

Our notions of the cosmos have evolved enormously over the past century. While everyone knows that the earth spins on its axis and orbits the sun, too few appreciate that the sun orbits the center of our galaxy (the Milky Way) and that there are a hundred billion such galaxies that are like small islands in a vast expanding sea of space. Taking a step back, fifty years ago, the number of people in cosmology could be counted on two hands. None of them could have predicted that the field would flourish as it has. There are now many thousands involved and the science is even presented in high school texts.

In fifty years, we hope that nonscientists will have as clear a picture of the large scale structure and workings of the universe as they have of the solar system today. One anticipates that such knowledge will permeate our society in ways perhaps not unlike Copernicus's insights.

In fifty years, I think that "fundamental" physics will be done differently. The past century has seen an amazing advance in our understanding of the fundamental building blocks of Nature. In most cases, the certainty of our knowledge is based on the ability to manipulate some aspect of Nature and then observe the consequences. In other words, on the ability do an experiment. A clear example of this is the science from particle accelerators or "atom smashers." Particles are collided untold numbers of times and we observe the consequences.

We will likely have new telescopes that routinely observe ripples in space time—gravitational waves—from colliding stars or black holes.

A new trend in science has begun to take hold and my guess is that it will be in full force in fifty years. More and more we look to the cosmos as passive observers to test fundamental notions of how Nature works. Our certainty that we truly understand something new and deep in Nature will come not from the ability to predict the outcome of an experiment whose settings we can adjust, but rather the certainty will come from a vast web of overlapping and interlocking passive observations that can be explained with only a limited number of assumptions (if we are lucky). This is a new way of doing fundamental science.

It is not difficult to imagine that in fifty years we will know the velocities and positions of all 100,000,000,000 galaxies in the observable universe. We will likely have new telescopes that routinely observe ripples in space time—

gravitational waves—from colliding stars or black holes. Others may be looking for gravitational waves from the big bang. There may also be multiple arrays of underground detectors catching new forms of matter as the earth sweeps through them in its orbit around the galactic center.

The technologies developed for these pursuits will find their ways into everyday life. Already we anticipate that we will be monitoring all nearby celestial objects to see if they will potentially crash into the earth. As another example, technologies for looking at the cosmos are already being harnessed to check that nuclear reactors are not producing weapons-grade materials.

One expects that the most scientifically rich fields in fifty years are in areas that have not been discovered or are now just barely recognized. Nevertheless, we can be sure that we will be enlightened through that indomitable aspect of the human spirit that drives us to search for new phenomena and to understand Nature more deeply.

52

Carol M. Browner

Carol M. Browner is the former administrator of the Environmental Protection Agency, where she championed common-sense, cost-effective solutions to the world's most pressing environmental and public health challenges. She is now a principal of The Albright Group LLC, a global strategy firm.

WE WILL HAVE LEARNED OUR LESSON

I have a lot of hope for what our world might be like fifty years from today. First and foremost, I believe we will have learned our lesson with regard to the harm caused by environmental inattention and inaction. We will no longer be electing leaders who believe that if we turn a blind eye to environmental problems, they will simply go away. In fifty years, we will have taken significant steps to address what I believe is the most pressing environmental and public health issue that our country, and for that matter the world, has ever faced: climate change.

I am optimistic that the United States will have realized its rightful place as a leader in protecting the health and sustainability of our planet. We will have passed national legislation to curb global warming—a measure that will cover virtually all human-caused sources of greenhouse gas emissions, that will be strong and enforceable, and that will include a national emissions credit trading program. The result will be a significant reduction in our country's greenhouse gas emissions.

We will finally join an international agreement on climate change. We'll no longer be the country dragging its feet and holding the rest of the world back. The world will have committed to cut global warming emissions by at least 80 to 90 percent in developed countries and by more than half worldwide.

In fifty years, we will also have learned that there is an economic upside to doing right by the environment. Though there will be costs associated with reducing emissions, those costs will be less than anticipated. American ingenuity will serve us well, and we will discover new ways to reduce our greenhouse gas emissions without undermining our economy. We will be less reliant on fossil fuels and more innovative in developing and marketing alternate sources of energy.

I am optimistic about the world we will have fifty years from now. Individuals, businesses, and countries across the globe will be doing their part for a clean, safe, and healthy planet. We will give this earth to our grandchildren the way it was given to us, so we are remembered for our responsibility—not cursed for our selfishness—by generations to come.

53

Richard Dawkins

Richard Dawkins, FRS, is an evolutionary biologist at the University of Oxford. He is the author of nine books, including The Selfish Gene *and* Unweaving the Rainbow.

The Future of the Soul

Fifty years on, science will have killed the soul. What a terrible, soulless thing to say! But only if you misunderstand it (easily done, admittedly). There are two meanings, Soul-1 and Soul-2, superficially confusable but deeply different. The following definitions from the *Oxford English Dictionary* convey what I am calling Soul-1:

> *The spiritual part of man regarded as surviving after death, and as susceptible of happiness or misery in a future state.*

> *The disembodied spirit of a deceased person regarded as a separate entity and as invested with some amount of form and personality.*

Soul-1, the soul that science is going to destroy, is supernatural, disembodied, survives the death of the brain, and is capable of happiness or misery even when the neurons are dust and the hormones dry. Science is going to kill it stone dead. Soul-2, however, will never be threatened by science. On the contrary, science is its twin and handmaiden. These definitions, also from the *Oxford English Dictionary*, convey various aspects of Soul-2:

> *Intellectual or spiritual power. High development of the mental faculties. Also, in somewhat weakened sense, deep feeling, sensitivity.*

> *The seat of the emotions, feelings, or sentiments; the emotional part of man's nature.*

Einstein was a great exponent of Soul-2 in science, and Carl Sagan was a virtuoso. *Unweaving the Rainbow* is my own modest celebration. Or listen to the great Indian astrophysicist Subrahmanyan Chandrasekhar:

> *This "shuddering before the beautiful," this incredible fact that a discovery motivated by a search after the beautiful in mathematics should find its exact replica in Nature, persuades me to say that beauty is that to which the human mind responds at its deepest and most profound.*

That was Soul-2, the kind of soulfulness that science courts and loves, and from which it will never be parted. The rest of this article refers only to Soul-1. Soul-1 is rooted in the dualistic theory that there is something nonmaterial about life, some nonphysical vital principle. It's the theory according to which a body has to be animated by an anima, vitalized by a vital force, energized by some mysterious energy, spiritualized by a spirit, made conscious by a mystical thing or substance called consciousness. It is no accident that all those characterizations of Soul-1 are circular. Julian Huxley memorably satirized Henri Bergson's '*élan vitale*' by suggesting that a railway engine works by *élan locomotif* (incidentally, it is a lamentable fact that Bergson is still the only scientist ever to win the Nobel Prize for literature). Science has already battered and wasted Soul-1. Within fifty years it will extinguish it altogether.

Fifty years back, we were only beginning to come to terms with Watson and Crick's 1953 paper in *Nature*, and few had tumbled to its poleaxing significance.

Theirs was seen as no more than a clever feat of molecular crystallography, while their last sentence ("It has not escaped our notice that the specific pairing we have postulated immediately suggests a possible copying mechanism for the genetic material") was just amusingly laconic understatement. With hindsight we can see that to call it understatement was itself the mother of understatements.

Before Watson/Crick (one contemporary scientist said to Crick, "But I thought your name was Watson-Crick") it was still possible for a leading historian of science, Charles Singer, to write:

> . . . *despite interpretations to the contrary, the theory of the gene is not a "mechanist" theory. The gene is no more comprehensible as a chemical or physical entity than is the cell or, for that matter, the organism itself . . . If I ask for a living chromosome, that is, for the only effective kind of chromosome, no one can give it to me except in its living surroundings any more than he can give me a living arm or leg. The doctrine of the relativity of functions is as true for the gene as it is for any of the organs of the body. They exist and function only in relation to other organs. Thus the last of the biological theories leaves us where the first started, in the presence of a power called life or psyche which is not only of its own kind but unique in each and all of its exhibitions.*[1]

Watson and Crick drove a coach and horses through all that: blew it ignominiously out of the water. Biology is becoming a branch of informatics. The Watson/Crick gene is a one-dimensional string of linear data, differing from a computer file only in the trivial respect that its universal code is quaternary, not binary. Genes are isolatable strings of digital data—they can be read out of living or dead bodies; they can be written on paper and stored in a library, ready to be used again at any time. It is already possible, though expensive, to write your entire genome in a book, and mine in an almost identical book. Fifty years hence, genomics will be so cheap that the library will house the complete genomes of as many thousands of species as we want. This will give us the final, definitive family tree of all life. Judicious comparison, in the library, of the genomes of any pair of modern species will allow us a fair shot at reconstruct-ing their extinct common ancestor, especially if we also throw into the compu-tational mix the genomes of its modern ecological counterparts. Embryological science will be so advanced that we'll be able to clone a living, breathing repre-sentative of that ancestor. Or of Lucy the Australopithecine, perhaps? Maybe even a dinosaur. And by 2058, it will be child's play to take down from its shelf the book that bears your name, type your genome back into a DNA synthesizer, insert it into an enucleated egg, and clone you—your identical twin but fifty years younger. Will it be a resurrection of your conscious being, a reincarnation of your subjectivity? No. We already know the answer is no, because monozy-gotic twins don't share a single subjective identity. They may have uncannily similar intuitions, but they do not think they are each other.

Just as Darwin in the mid-nineteenth century destroyed the mystical "design" argument, and just as Watson and Crick in the mid-twentieth century destroyed all mystical nonsense about genes, their successors of the mid-twenty-first cen-tury will destroy the mystical absurdity of souls being detached from bodies. It won't be easy. Subjective consciousness is undeniably mysterious. In *How the Mind Works*, Steven Pinker elegantly sets out the problem of consciousness, and asks where it comes from and what the explanation is. Then he's frank enough to say, "Beats the heck out of me." That's honest, and I echo it. We don't know. We don't understand it. Yet. But I believe we will, some time before 2058. And if we do, it certainly won't be mystics or theologians who solve this greatest of all riddles but scientists—maybe a lone genius like Darwin, but more probably a combination of neuroscientists, computer scientists, and science-savvy philoso-phers. Soul-1 will die a belated and unlamented death at the hand of science, which will in the process launch Soul-2 to undreamed-of heights.

54

Peter Marra

*Peter Marra is a research scientist at the Smithsonian Migratory Bird
Center of the National Zoological Park and a leading researcher in the
area of migratory bird ecology.*

A Bird's-Eye View of the Next 50 Years

I typically leave predictions of the future to astrologers and weathermen. But
as I consider that I have two small children who will be fifty-six and fifty-two
in fifty years, it seems a reasonable exercise to consider the ecological conditions under which they will be living.

Since the early age of five, I knew I wanted to study animals. I spent every
waking hour flipping rocks for salamanders, setting traps for rabbits, catching
frogs and turtles, and watching birds. This passion ultimately turned into my
career, although most of my energies today are directed at studying the lives
of migratory birds. As I edge (moving more quickly each year it seems) toward
fifty, I remain as curious and as passionate today as I did as a child. For this
short essay, I will draw from my experiences as an ornithologist, an ecologist,
and a conservation biologist to examine the past fifty years and to use this
analysis to speculate on what the next fifty years might bring.

During the past fifty years we have changed the earth's environment at an
amazing rate. We have transformed our native habitat to suburban and urban

land cover at a rate of approximately 365 acres per hour, continued to emit harmful chemicals into our environment—resulting in genetic mutations, endocrine disruptors, and other unforeseen impacts—depleted native fish species such as the Atlantic cod and swordfish, and contributed to the decline of several species of migratory songbirds. We have also moved pathogens such as West Nile virus, avian influenza, and malaria around the globe, many inadvertently through trade.

Due largely to human influence, during the last half century the earth has experienced a general increase in mean surface air temperatures by about 0.5°C with warmer temperatures at temperate latitudes. This global climate change is rapidly melting glaciers, increasing the number of severe storms and droughts, and adversely impacting plant and animal communities around the world.

Due to several factors, bird populations, in particular, have declined and in some cases even gone extinct. Globally, there are approximately 9,775 bird species, and recent estimates project that 1,212 of these are threatened with extinction. That is roughly one-fifth of all extant bird species. Our ability to identify the *specific* factors impacting bird populations is limited, but it is clear that the development activities mentioned above are primarily responsible. The elimination of native habitat such as forests and grasslands is thought to be a primary driver in the decline of many songbird populations.

Some scientists estimate that we may lose 10 percent or more of our bird species in the next fifty years.

Overfishing of key prey fish and the direct mortality caused by the long-lining fishing industries has taken a significant toll on seabirds. Trade and its role in the accidental introduction of pathogens such as avian malaria and West Nile virus around the world, including into the United States, has resulted in the complete extinction of some bird species on islands and severe reductions in population sizes of several bird species on mainland areas. Finally, birds in particular have exhibited a variety of responses to our changing climate, including earlier breeding, range extensions, and mistimed life history events.

What is not clear is how these agents of global change will continue to impact bird populations in the future. The trajectory we are on is clearly not good. Some scientists estimate that we may lose 10 percent or more of our bird species in the next fifty years. Although such predictions are not precise, they should be viewed as conservative to ensure maximum biodiversity protection. Our ability to predict what will happen in the next fifty years with species such as birds depends, in part, on our ability to identify how and the degree to which each of these and other factors cause bird populations to decline or increase. Currently, we have only a rudimentary understanding of the factors that limit and ultimately regulate populations of birds. Such an understanding is vital to our ability to protect populations of these wonderful animals from precipitous declines or even extinctions.

Many other ecological questions remain in part because of technological limitations. In the next fifty years, I predict that technological advances will allow us to make enormous strides in our understanding of the natural world—including, for example, identifying the specific geographic areas to and from which individual birds migrate. Currently, for most animals, we do not know where individual migratory animals spend their entire annual cycle. Not knowing where a particular species spends its entire annual cycle greatly impedes our ability to fully protect the species, comprehend most aspects of its ecology and evolution, and understand its ability to contribute to, for example, the movement of infectious disease. The problem lies in the fact that the animals themselves are too small and the spaces they traverse too large for current technology. I believe in the next fifty years this technology will develop, providing answers to many critical questions about migration and the animals that exhibit this spectacular behavior.

Limitations in technology, of course, remain only one of the major challenges to ensuring that the ecological conditions under which our children's, and their children's, lives are not bleak. The political will to address these challenges is, perhaps, our largest impediment to overcome in the next fifty years.

Perhaps technological advances during the past fifty years, such as the personal computer, the Internet, space travel, etc., which enhance our ability to communicate and perceive the world as interconnected, will increase our willingness to act to protect the environment. I sincerely hope so. Of course, the flip side of this coin is also critical to recognize—that many of these technological advances will also enhance our ability to continue to exploit and harm the earth's resources.

I want my grandchildren to experience nature as I have experienced nature. If the political will exists to protect our environment in the next fifty years, I am optimistic that this will be the case. Ecosystems and their species are resilient. Restoration ecologists and endangered species biologists have shown us that species and their habitats can be brought back from the brink. Striped Bass, Kirtland's Warblers, and Black-footed Ferrets are all excellent examples of species that have teetered on the edge but have rebounded with strength.

I want my grandchildren to experience nature as I have experienced nature.

Human society is learning to respond to the environmental crisis we have created somewhat inadvertently. Some changes are happening but they are not happening fast enough. We need an increase in a commitment to science education and introducing children to their natural environment as part of everyday curriculum. Humans are smart animals—but are we smart enough to avoid the ultimate irony contributing to our own extinction? Where will we be in fifty years? We will be where we choose to be. I am choosing to work hard to protect our natural environment so that my children and their children can experience the outdoors as I did.

55

Nsedu Obot-Witherspoon

*Nsedu Obot-Witherspoon is executive director of The Children's
Environmental Health Network, a national nonprofit organization whose
mission is to protect the child and the fetus from environmental health
hazards and promote a healthy environment.*

GLOBAL CLIMATE CHANGE AND OUR CHILDREN

I see the following vision for the next fifty years.

Global climate change is currently viewed by many in the public health community as the largest environmental health-related issue of our time. With the most recent International Panel on Climate Change report, there is near scientific unanimity that global climate change is occurring, that it is caused and/or exacerbated by human activities, and that the effects on human health and well-being are potentially very serious. In these reports, children are noted as particularly vulnerable. However, their vulnerabilities and specific health outcomes have not yet been fully characterized in a dedicated report or document. Policymakers in the United States do not have a full understanding of the enormous impact global climate change can have on the health of children nationally and worldwide.

We know that some of the major direct health effects of global climate change include: 1) Casualties and trauma during floods, typhoons, storms, hurricanes, and other natural disasters; and 2) Increased morbidity and mortality due to ischemic heart disease, respiratory disease, and disease of the nervous system, kidneys, etc., during hot weather. Indirect health effects include: 1) Increased incidence of infectious and parasitogenic diseases due to increased rainfalls; 2) Higher risk of intestinal infections due to the breakdown of water supply and sanitation networks; and 3) Increased morbidity and mortality from suspended particulates in air and other air pollutants during forest fires. Worldwide other issues such as forced migration, increased famine, poverty, crime, food security, and limited access to resources including arable land and water will have an impact on all members of society. All of these potential effects have enormous outcomes for children today as well as fifty years from now.

Regarding some of the traditional children's environmental health issues, I expect we will see a decrease in childhood lead poisoning due to further decay of older housing stock built before the 1970s and public awareness campaigns outlining the links to lead poisoning and lead paint exposure. Unfortunately, we will see increased cancer diagnosis, and childhood cancers specifically. A large reason for

Unfortunately, we will see increased cancer diagnosis, and childhood cancers specifically.

this trend will continue to be the use of pesticides in agricultural communities, exposing first the workers, who then track the chemicals home to their families. We will continue to see more relationships between emerging science and health outcomes particularly related to the asthma and obesity epidemic.

We will soon approach a time where universal health-care coverage will be the only option to increasing health-care costs, longevity of the aging, and severity of health ailments. I believe the development of a health tracking registry for both asthma and learning disabilities is vital and inevitable. Population diversity will be a great benefit and reality, enhancing the overall way that we view and interact with each other. Children of all economic backgrounds, ethnicities, and geography will benefit from a variety of pediatric environmental health research that will be translated for the general public.

Specifically, the National Children's Study will provide us with an incredible amount of childhood and environmental health linkages like we have never had the benefit of witnessing before. I propose that the current study will go so well that subsequent studies will soon follow.

Children are our future, but, unfortunately, if we continue on the various paths listed above, fifty years from now younger generations will continue to live more and more unhealthy lives when compared to the generations before them.

56

William H. Meadows

Bill Meadows is president of The Wilderness Society, whose mission is to protect and conserve America's wilderness and roadless areas, including the Arctic National Wildlife Refuge and national forests.

A Way Back to Wilderness

America is a nation forged out of the chaos of the wilderness. As the pioneers pushed to civilize a landscape with seemingly limitless horizons, laying waste to the untamed forests of the East and vast Western prairies, they reshaped a country and the lives of its native peoples. Ironically, the wilderness they subdued was also the primary source of sustenance for their precarious lives. Still, the destruction continued and has persisted unabated for almost two and a half centuries.

Most of our wilderness has vanished by now and the portion that remains exists primarily in congressionally designated areas within the federal public land system. The collapse of these essential landscapes is both the legacy of unchecked development and a sign of who we have become. In our careless enthusiasm to conquer the wilderness, we abandoned our relationship with the land and lost our bearings as responsible citizens in the community of life.

My dream is that one-half century from today we will have found our way again and reemerged as a nation fully committed to protecting its wild land heritage—an aspiration not beyond our reach. History has shown us the transforming power of an idea whose time has come.

The civil rights movement experienced a defining moment in August 1963, when Martin Luther King Jr. stood on the steps of the Lincoln Memorial and evoked his dream of equality and justice in America. No doubt the collective consciousness shifted that summer afternoon as countless African Americans found new hope for the future and began to think differently about their place in it.

In fifty years—as we pass the midpoint of the twenty-first century—I believe the American people will have embraced a new consciousness about the natural world, one as radically different from the past as the emancipation of hearts and minds from unquestioned racism in the 1960s and as comprehensive as shuttering the last whites-only diner. We might look back on these days at the dawn of the new century and wonder if 2007 was the tipping point, the pivotal moment when a shift in environmental thinking took root.

Climate change has changed us. There is perhaps no starker example of our disengagement from the natural world than global warming. With evidence mounting that carbon emissions were undermining the health of the planet, we blithely continued to feed our reckless energy addiction. Not surprising, since few could remember a time when anything from nature touched their stressed out, vacuum-sealed lives. (If there was a link between human beings and the natural world, it probably was packaged and sitting on the grocery store shelf.) Fewer still took any personal actions to address the climate problem, complacently sitting by as our lifeboat sprang leaks.

But a funny thing happened on the way to disaster. Try as we might, the massive amount of data about the worldwide impact of global warming was simply too pervasive to ignore. No longer blameless innocents, people from every walk of life suddenly started to accept their complicity in the issue of climate change. If a full-blown national conservation ethic was not born the night Al Gore's documentary *An Inconvenient Truth* won an Academy Award, certainly the seeds of such a possibility were sown. Millions of new activists blossomed almost overnight.

For those of us who love wilderness, this sea change in attitude signaled a teaching moment, the rare opportunity to talk about humanity's indissoluble links to the natural world. With the window on global warming flung wide open, people could see how the tentacles of their environmental decisions grew and spread, invading even the most hidden corners of the planet.

This was the moment when, in the words of the conservation giant Aldo Leopold, our country had the opportunity to embrace a new ethical imperative toward the environment. I am convinced that capturing the magic of this moment will create the medium for action. "All ethics," Leopold noted, "rest upon a single premise: that the individual is a member of a community of interdependent parts . . . The land ethic simply enlarges the boundaries of the community to include soils, waters, plants and animals—or collectively, the land."

Therein lies the conservation movement's single most important aspiration for 2050 and beyond: to experience a foundational shift in the collective consciousness of this country, which manifests in faithful respect for the earth and each other.

It is a new vision for America. We picture a world where preserving wildness has become a core concern for our people who actively work to sustain it across the landscape. "Green" has gone mainstream, and voters regularly support candidates who endorse conservation. No longer dependent on fossil fuels, we are the new American pioneers who have explored the uncharted territories of renewable energy and carbon footprints and found solutions in mitigation, alternative energy, carbon sequestration, and transformed lifestyles. The global warming crisis has been averted.

The fundamental body of policies, laws, and budget practices affecting our land base reflect a clear charge: first, protect the resource. Local governments, from small towns to state capitals, have made the preservation of wild places a priority. They honor the legacy of the land and set business and zoning regulations accordingly.

Species no longer go extinct, because wild creatures have sufficient habitat and freedom of movement to thrive. From forest to ocean, vigorous populations of native plants and animals flourish in vast protected ecosystems. A

nationwide network of wild lands—with 200 million acres of federally designated wilderness at its heart—sustains wildness across America.

Visitors from 2007 looking down from space would notice a remarkable
change in the landscape. It is green. A complex web of natural areas stretches
from the northern tip of Maine to Baja, California, the Arctic Circle to the
Florida Keys. This continuum of wildness sweeps from parks in urban city
centers through suburban open spaces, municipal greenways, rural enclaves,
scenic rivers, wildlife habitat corridors, state conservation sites, and on to pristine wilderness areas.

Countless acres are physically connected; countless others form a tapestry that
has been woven together by the threads of migrating wildlife. Culture, tradition,
and recreation link them all to the hearts of the American people. Interlaced
among this ever-expanding mosaic are prospering communities whose citizens
are committed to sustaining natural systems. They know a healthy environment
is essential to a robust economy and consider it a civic duty to care for the land.

In our world, wildness endures. Streams run pure from mountain head-
waters to rivers below, nourishing the land and all who depend upon it. It is a
world where human beings assume their roles as equal citizens in the great
community of life, knowing that they are inextricably linked to the natural
world—a connection that begins at the threshold of each home and extends
in all directions through neighborhoods and towns, across artificial boundaries, and on to the fields, forests, mountains, deserts, and rivers that are the
common concern of all.

57

Lawrence M. Krauss

Lawrence M. Krauss is a theoretical physicist and director of the Center for Education and Research in Cosmology and Astrophysics at Case Western Reserve University. He is the author of numerous bestselling books, including The Physics of Star Trek, Atom, *and, most recently,* Hiding in the Mirror.

FUTURE WORLD: THE BAD, THE GOOD, AND THE UGLY

Predictions about the future have a habit of being wrong, because they tend to miss the unexpected but profoundly new developments that change the way humans behave, such as the development of the Internet in the 1980s. Nevertheless, borrowing shamelessly from Charles Dickens, I feel confident that the future will be both the best of times and the worst of times.

I will organize my predictions around a variety of themes, and subthemes, centered around the Bad, the Good, and the Ugly.

The Bad:

1. Global Warming: All evidence not only suggests that human-induced global warming is real, but that we are rapidly approaching a time when

we will be living on a planet that is fundamentally different than the planet life has flourished on over the past 500,000 years. There will be dramatic climate changes that will raise water levels by meters at least over the next fifty years, displacing perhaps one billion people who live near sea level in the poorest countries in the world. The direct impact of global warming on more northern (and southern) climes is less clear. There is no doubt that some areas will benefit, by increased agricultural output, but the pressures put on the first world by the devastation that will be wrought in the third world will be immense.

2. Energy: The next fifty years will be the period during which the source of the world's power needs will, of necessity, shift from oil and gas to something else. I anticipate that technology will meet the challenge of finding new, renewable, energy sources. However, the challenge to power the world of 2058 will nevertheless be daunting, and the transition will be rocky. With a global population in excess of ten billion people, the power requirements to allow all of humanity to achieve a standard of living that approaches that now enjoyed in the West would require a new Gigawatt power plant to come online every day for over forty years. That will not happen. Either we will dramatically learn how to reduce our net energy consumption, or we can expect that the world will divide into the energy-have nations and the energy-have-not nations, whose GNPs will reflect this divide.

3. Nuclear Terrorism and Nuclear War: The world has lasted sixty years without the use of nuclear weapons in wartime, since the explosions at Nagasaki and Hiroshima. Yet the superpowers possess over twenty thousand nuclear weapons and they are proliferating throughout the world. It is thus hard to conceive that terrorists will at some point not gain access to even a rudimentary nuclear weapon, which they will then use. Such an explosion will not destroy humanity, but whether it could serve as the spark of a larger nuclear war is not clear.

The Good

1. Medicine and Our Scientific Understanding of Life: It has been said that the twenty-first century will be the century of biology, as the twentieth was for physics. In fact, I think the two fields will largely merge, as we begin to understand the processes that power life at the atomic and molecular levels. I am confident that we will not only understand the origin of life, and recreate it in the laboratory within fifty years, but also that we will completely redefine what life is, controlling many of the processes that govern the way we survive as individuals and a species. Medicine will conquer many existing diseases and extend the human lifespan considerably. These developments will, of course, have profound social and ethical impacts, and how we handle these will determine whether the future will resemble *Brave New World,* or *Star Trek.*

2. Computer Intelligence: I see no obstacle to continued improvements in computer technology, leading ultimately to intelligent, self-aware machines. Unlike Ray Kurzweil, I doubt this will happen within thirty years, but fifty years is a possibility. Once this happens, the future of intelligence on Earth will be forever changed. Intelligent, self-programmable machines will undoubtedly be able to develop much faster than biological systems, so to adapt we will have to incorporate machine intelligence into what it means to be human, or we will be left behind. This may sound like a scary future, sort of like the Borg on *Star Trek,* but I don't think it has to be. The result could be a profoundly improved species and a safer planet. We will see.

3. Virtual Reality: Our ability to manipulate artificial environments, either on massively parallel computers or using 3D holographic technologies, will continue to improve exponentially. We are already seeing artificial worlds like Second Life, where people meet, buy land, have sex, etc. I think these worlds will become more and more attractive, realistic, and addictive, and I expect there will be individuals within fifty years who will do most of their living in these environments.

Whether or not one views this as "good" depends upon one's perspective, but nevertheless, I think it will happen.

The Ugly:

The Struggle between Science and Religion: There has been an inherent tension between these two different realms of the human intellectual experience for over a thousand years, both in the West and the East. In the twelfth century in the Islamic world, for example, evolving theology effectively killed a burgeoning scientific and mathematical culture, while in Europe the Catholic Church effectively repressed scientific inquiry during the Middle Ages. In the United States, there has been a growing fundamentalist movement opposed to the teaching of science, especially evolution, in our schools. Many individuals trained at so-called institutions of higher education, like Liberty University, which are in reality bastions of fundamentalism, now hold positions of some influence in Washington. At the same time, a resurgence of Islamic Fundamentalism, fueled no doubt in part as a reaction of technologically impoverished societies to the wealth and power of the non-Islamic Western cultures, also is working effectively to fight the propagation of knowledge. The question that naturally arises is whether these forces of ignorance will prevail during the next fifty years or whether scientific progress will continue unscathed. There are reasons for optimism. The intelligent design movement in the United States has, for example, had several serious setbacks over the past year or two. However, the United States tends to export all aspects of its culture, both good and bad, and there are rising anti-intellectual forces in Europe. I expect that the current ongoing battle between Islam and Christianity and between fundamentalism of all sorts of rationalism will worsen in the near term. The huge global technological challenges facing humanity, with rising populations, energy crises, and global warming, will exacerbate these tensions. The resulting world fifty years from now will depend on how humanity emerges from these battles.

58

John C. Mather

Dr. John C. Mather, who shares the 2006 Nobel Prize in Physics with George Smoot, is a senior astrophysicist in the Observational Cosmology Laboratory at NASA's Goddard Space Flight Center. He is senior project scientist of the James Webb Space Telescope.

ALWAYS SO MUCH MORE TO DISCOVER

At this point in human history, we are witnessing a nexus of scientific collaboration and advanced technology that promises to give rise to an explosion in knowledge that is, in both the literal and figurative senses of the phrase, earth shattering. Astrophysics already has begun to measure the infant universe. Scientists are regularly engaged in discovering more about dark matter—matter not directly detected or observed, but rather inferred from gravitational effects on visible matter and responsible for shaping the galaxies—and dark energy, the form of energy responsible not only for speeding up the universe but shaping galaxies within it. In very simple terms, today we have remarkable insights into where we came from and where we are going.

In the next fifty years, there is every reason to believe these insights will move rapidly toward even greater definition. With the launch of the James Webb Space Telescope, projected for 2013, we may well actually witness planetary formation, until now not visible because we have not had as much capacity to work in the infrared range of the electromagnetic spectrum. Imagine literally tracing the connection of the Milky Way to our solar system, reaching back through millions of years to witness a cosmic fireworks display as stars erupt.

We fully expect within the next two decades to find earthlike planets elsewhere in the galaxy.

We fully expect within the next two decades to find earthlike planets elsewhere in the galaxy.

Aside from the thrilling advance in what we know about the origin of the universe, we can expect equally exciting progress in what we know about where we go from here and how fast. Cosmology, like some of the other sciences, directs our attention away from the next fiscal year, the next election cycle, the next generation, even the next century to a longer-range vision. Unfortunately, our media is far more likely to report on fights than on facts. Cosmological research can change that perspective, an important contribution no matter what is actually discovered.

When I look back at the Apollo mission, I am astonished at the accomplishments. Today it's difficult to fathom, but those hardy individuals basically worked with slide rules. Space travel then and now is far more difficult than people like to admit. And there is a substantial discrepancy between dreams and reality. The science fiction idea of space stations that support billions of people is simply wishful thinking. The crucial point, though, is that if we do indeed accomplish what we think we might—launch and sustain a telescope that will pour brand new data into our research, isolate a dark matter particle in the lab, create a conscious machine as artificial intelligence guru Ray Kurzweil suggests—we will have unexpected ways of improving the future. While space stations can't yet produce the water and air and food humans must have, they can be great laboratories for learning how to do it, and they may well be optimal environments for human-directed machines.

All of this, of course, is subject to decisions made outside the scientific arena. I recently visited Alexandria, Egypt. Standing there, recalling the great library of the ancient world, and how its existence and its loss affected the progress of knowledge, I was struck by the recognition that once again, we could well lose our way. Knowledge today is more widely dispersed than it was then. Our world is dependent on the currency of commercial success. We at NASA understand the need for public scrutiny, and see our job as not just accomplishing what many insist is an all but impossible mission, but making sure the world at large knows what we are doing and why.

Those of us in the United States are particularly fortunate. From its inception, this country has known leaders who were at least interested in science, and many quite adept. Benjamin Franklin and Thomas Jefferson are, of course, the paradigmatic early instances. Today, we work in a world of lively collaboration, greatly enhanced by the fact that our colleagues from other countries want to come here. And, yes, there is still competition, and that is, in fact, a good thing. The Cold War was a source of significant support for science, and now public concern with climate change has turned the spotlight our way again.

What we must remember is that whatever extraordinary tools we have at our disposal in fifty years, whatever horizons we peer into and beyond, we guarantee our future by making this country, this world, a good place to be.

59

Ahmed Zewail

Ahmed Zewail was awarded the 1999 Nobel Prize in Chemistry for his pioneering development in femtoscience, making possible the observation of phenomena in a millionth of a billionth of a second. He is chair professor of chemistry and physics and director of the Center for Physical Biology at Caltech. Postage stamps have been issued to honor his contributions to science and humanity.

THE WORLD IN FIFTY YEARS: REVOLUTIONS AND REPERCUSSIONS

Traveling through time is a real challenge. Throughout history, predictions of the future have been claimed by notables and later proved to be contrary to reality. We usually think in the frame of reference of the "present" without, for most people, being able to see into the "future"—crystal balls do not usually work. The founder of IBM, Thomas J. Watson, about the future of computers said in 1943, "I think there is a world market for about five computers." Multiply this number by a billion to reach the reality of our time! Nevertheless, it is interesting to conjecture the state of the twenty-first century because of its uniqueness in the history of human knowledge. In the coming fifty years, any analysis of the state of progress must consider forces of knowledge and faith, affected, of course, by the political, economic, and natural changes of influence.

There is no doubt that one can predict, based on current trends, that science and technology will provide new discoveries and innovations in many fields of endeavor. Here, I first highlight advances that will span vast scales of length and time—from the micro, very small (atomic scale), to the macro, very big (cosmos scale), and to the very complex (life), the scale in between. For the micro world, it will become possible to tame and manipulate matter on the nanometer (a billionth of a meter) length scale and on the femtosecond to attosecond (a millionth of a billionth, and a billionth of a billionth, respectively) timescale. This control with precision may lead to the synthesis of robotic micro-machines that can form "intelligent matter," matter with a specific molecular-scale function, or the building of a biological-mimic factory, the cell. Drug design from first principles would have a huge impact on the cure of diseases, hopefully at much reduced prices for the needy, especially those in less developed countries. Academically, such multidisciplinary approaches, requiring knowledge of various physical and biological sciences, will restructure university education and redefine new fields of study at the interface.

Building on advances in molecular and cellular developments, humankind will reach a far better understanding of the biological function of organs, such as the brain, but I doubt that the code of consciousness will be cracked even in fifty years of research. New tools will be developed to observe the behavior of complex systems in space and time, and new concepts describing complexity may emerge. Treatment of diseases such as Alzheimer's will take a new course— control at the level of the molecule (protein); the targeting of genes (DNA); or the making of spare parts organs using stem cells and cloning techniques aided by current methods of genetic engineering, molecular biology, and gene expression (PCR, RNAi, recombinant DNA . . .). In the coming fifty years, life spans may extend beyond one hundred years, and human health care will shift more from the office of physicians toward homes in what I call "PM care," or personal medicine. But medical and societal benefits will not evolve without some repercussions. The synthesis or control of physical matter is vastly different from the interference with or modification of life (e.g., using silicon instead of carbon as a base), and to many on this planet this intrusion represents a conflict with religious belief. Without improved education and open discourse on ethics and morality, clashes of science and society may become of serious consequence, even in developed countries such as the United States.

Progress will not only be made in the world of matter and life, but also in the cosmos at large. More than 80 percent of our universe is made of dark energy, and we at present do not really understand its nature. The physical observed matter is only about 5 percent and the rest is dark matter—matter of unknown composition, which cannot be observed optically, but whose presence is inferred from the effect of gravity on visible matter. In this century, cosmology as a science will provide a better understanding of dark energy and matter. We may also uncover some mysteries of black holes by detecting gravity waves, hopefully with new surprises beyond the predictions of Einstein's general theory of relativity. Space missions will continue to explore the solar system and beyond, and we may learn more about the involvement of planets in the origin-of-life question. Colonies may be formed on the Moon—hopefully not for military purposes— and commercial spaceship travel may become the new Dreamland, the Disneyland that people will enjoy trekking to, but at a price!

In technology, it is safe to say that the most rapidly changing development will be that of information and computers. The leaps forward will result from the reduction of the physical size of computers and the increase in their computation capacity and speed, possibly beyond the limit of (Gordon) Moore's Law—an empirical observation in 1965 that held that the number of transistors on a single chip (integrated circuit) will double nearly every two years. The expansion of the wideband network and the integration of multimedia into one device, not to mention the possibility of quantum computing using the language of the atom (quantum mechanics), will have a major impact on information communication, speed and capacity, and on society and culture. Society will readjust to the information explosion, but we should expect that traditional family values may be further compromised.

Unfortunately, despite these anticipated discoveries and innovations, there are daunting chasms to cross in the coming fifty years. Advanced, and even simple, technologies will empower some people to inflict large-scale disasters through "terrorist acts" or "freedom-fighting causes." Given the 80 percent population of the have-nots on our planet, a large fraction of people are desperate or frustrated because of their poor economic or unfavorable political situation, and they will somehow blow off their steam and unleash significant damages in large-scale populations. Chemical, biological, or nuclear weapons, such as dirty bombs, may be used, and, as a result, the response may trigger the first big nuclear war between nations. It would be wise to alleviate, or at least ease, the despair of the have-nots, and to sustain economic and education aid guided by bridging dialogues, especially between the West and the 1.3 billion Muslims. Judging from the performance of today's world leaders, and despite human progress, I fear the continuing dearth of visionary solutions to the underlying causes of human misery—ignorance and deprivation.

In the coming fifty years, the only superpower of today's world may have real competition, and the challenges are both international and national. In an interdependent world, the United States can no longer afford to have a fragmented and incoherent foreign policy. As other nations build up to a leading economic position, the United States cannot allow the erosion of innovation and investment in R/D, decline in work ethics, and the weakening of the traditionally powerful middle class. As importantly, the unique value system that guided the nation and attracted the best minds from around the world cannot be convoluted by the political gains of elected officials and lobbyists. All of these factors will determine the global position of the United States in fifty years. Already economic indicators forecast that by 2050, China will have a projected GDP of $45 trillion, surpassing the United States, with India's GDP approaching that of the United States, and the dollar is losing its prime position among all currencies. I, however, still believe in the American

> *Despite human progress, I fear the continuing dearth of visionary solutions to the underlying causes of human misery—ignorance and deprivation.*

system for creativity, and hopefully in the coming fifty years the country will restructure its political and education systems to preserve the values that defined its uniqueness in history.

The above exposé into science, technology, and society does not take into account natural forces that bring about disasters. These include consequences of climate change, major epidemics or earthquakes, hurricanes such as Katrina, and possibly a 50–100 km asteroid impacting the earth in an unprecedented collision. Surprises such as 9/11, Hiroshima's mass destruction, or a viral/mechanical breakdown of e-communication may occur before fifty years. But one major force beyond nature that is surely here to stay is religion. It would be naïve to ignore the importance of faith in the lives of billions of people all over the globe. In fifty years' time, many of the troubles that currently plague the world can be considerably mitigated if, in the vision of policy and diplomacy, we accept reason and faith, which need not be in conflict, as the dual human need for knowledge and meaning of life on this planet.

In closing, I believe that the coming fifty years will bring about revolutionary discoveries and innovations as humankind acquires new knowledge. Humans, however, are still the same species—Homo sapiens—that desire the use of force in all forms, as primitive as fire and as sophisticated as nuclear bombs. What is different in the twenty-first century is the ability of a few individuals to cause massive destruction. It is clear, at least to me, that in the coming fifty years and beyond, the picture is, on one hand, rosy for the scientific and medical advances that will positively transform lives, and, on the other hand, gloomy when considering the lack of vision in global affairs. Progress can only be realized when political leaders see the world through the lens of human rights and peaceful coexistence. Only then can the new generations fully benefit from the tremendous potential of the twenty-first century.

60

Ross Gelbspan

Ross Gelbspan was an editor and reporter for thirty years with the
Philadelphia Bulletin, *the* Washington Post, *and the* Boston Globe,
where he won a Pulitzer Prize for editing in 1994. He is the author of
two books on the global climate, The Heat Is On *and* Boiling Point.
Now retired from daily journalism, Gelbspan is the creator and author of
the Website www.heatisonline.org.

THE EARTH IN 50 YEARS: RESCUE . . . OR RUIN?

In fifty years, we could be living in a world in which global cooperation has replaced global competition as the dominant dynamic, in which we have shed the increasingly artificial national allegiances that divide us, and in which people all over the world have come together in a common worldwide project to rescue a severely distressed planet.

Alternatively, we could be struggling to survive a desolate and long-lasting era of climate hell.

There seems no doubt that portions of the global infrastructure will, at the very least, have been profoundly disrupted by the dramatic increase in extreme weather events. The warming of the atmosphere is already destroying forests in Alaska as well as in the northwestern United States and Canada. We will likely be seeing crop failures in the world's "breadbaskets" due to changes in rainfall patterns, more extensive drought, water scarcity, and insect infestations.

> *We will likely be seeing crop failures in the world's "breadbaskets" due to changes in rainfall patterns, more extensive drought, water scarcity, and insect infestations.*

They will be accompanied by a corresponding increase in number of insect-borne diseases—malaria, dengue fever, yellow fever, and Lyme disease. And we will witness significant declines in fish and shellfish harvests—both because of overfishing and also because of the acidification of the world's oceans from the fallout of our carbon emissions.

Many of these impacts will almost certainly begin to occur within the next half century.

Carbon dioxide, the major heat-trapping gas released by our burning of coal and oil, stays in the atmosphere for about one hundred years. So even if we were to replace all our coal-fired generating plants, our oil-burning furnaces, and our gasoline-burning cars today, we would still be subject to a long period of costly and traumatic weather extremes.

The world will most likely reflect other changes that transcend the impacts of a more erratic weather regime. For one example, as the ice caps in the Arctic regions melt, they not only contribute more water to rising sea levels but they also are upsetting the planet's heat balance. Earth's traditional ice cover has, for millennia, reflected a certain amount of sunlight back into space, acting as a stabilizing element in the planet's thermostat. But as that ice cover disappears, it not only reflects less heat back into the atmosphere, it also allows much more heat to be absorbed by the land and ocean areas it previously covered.

The real question is not so much what our world will look like in fifty years. In the last several years, three extremely prominent scientists—Dr. Rajendra Pachauri, chair of the Intergovernmental Panel on Climate Change; Dr. James Hansen of NASA; and James Lovelock, the renowned British ecologist—have all declared that we are either very close to, or have already passed, a point of no return in terms of staving off major climate impacts.

The real question is how we as a species will respond to these changes.

The most likely—but not inevitable—response will be a totalitarian one. When governments are confronted by breakdowns, their most likely response is to use their police and military power to restore or impose order. New Orleans mayor Ray Nagin was certainly no dictator. But when Katrina—and its torrential aftermath—inundated entire neighborhoods, the mayor was forced to bring in the National Guard to enforce evacuation orders, clear escape routes, and try to limit the predictable outbreak of looting and lawlessness. On a larger scale, it is not hard to foresee governments resorting to permanent states of martial law in countries whose crops are destroyed by weather extremes, whose lands are going under from rising sea levels, and whose borders are overrun by environmental refugees.

History's hopeful news is that rapid social change can erupt as rapidly and unexpectedly as rapid climate change. The Berlin Wall came down in about two years. Apartheid in South Africa was overturned in the historical blink of an eye.

It is just possible that, given the gathering and increasingly unmistakable signs of the onset of climate chaos, people will begin to focus more on our similarities than on our differences. At the most concrete level, nature is telling us that we need to join together in a common global project to change our energy infrastructures—away from coal and oil and to non-carbon energy sources like wind, solar, small-scale hydropower, wave and tidal power, and other less destructive forms of energy.

A global energy transition would create millions of jobs, especially in developing countries.

A global energy transition would create millions of jobs, especially in developing countries. It could turn impoverished and dependent countries into trading partners. It could raise living standards abroad without compromising ours. It could undermine the economic desperation that gives rise to so much anti-US sentiment. And in a very short time, it could jump the renewable energy industry into a central, driving engine of growth of the global economy.

Stepping back for a moment to a wider-angle vantage point, this kind of initiative could also be the beginning of the end of an outdated and increasingly toxic nationalism that we have long ago outgrown.

The economy is becoming truly globalized.

The globalization of communications now makes it possible for any person to communicate with anyone else around the world.

And since it is no respecter of national boundaries, the global climate makes us one.

Our modern history has been marked by a dichotomy between the totalitarianism of command-and-control economies and the opulence and brutality of unregulated markets and runaway globalization. It is just possible that a global public works project to rewire the planet could serve as a model that could begin to point us all toward that optimal calibration of competition and cooperation that would maximize our energy and creativity and productivity while, at the same time, dramatically extending the baseline conditions for peace—peace among people and peace between people and nature.

That is the most optimistic scenario. It is not the most likely. In the past, when nature and history have collided, nature has always won—and history has always had to start back over again.

The next half century will tell us in many ways how much we have learned from the last half century.

Acknowledgments

Putting this book together was a team effort.

Our thanks to Bill Adler, who had the idea, and to Bill Adler Jr., Peggy Robin, Jeanne Welsh, Rachael Garrity, Deb Sherer, April Moore, and Katrina Milligan of Adler & Robin Books who were invaluable in securing the material.

We are grateful for the encouragement and support of our publisher, especially David Moberg, Joel Miller, and Kristen Parrish.

We acknowledge the assistance of Mel Berger at the William Morris Agency, Jayme Brown in Mike Wallace's office, and Mary Wallace for her enthusiasm for the book.

We thank them all. They made this book possible.

Notes

Chapter 14

1. Dr. Lane Neal, Science and Technology Speech, The Secretary of State's Open Forum Conversation Series, Washington DC (June 22, 2000), Transcript, accessed March 26, 2007, http://www.ostp.gov/html/00727.html.

2. United Nations, *World Population Prospects, The 2006 Revision* (ESA/WP.202), (New York: Department of Economics and Social Affairs, Population Division, 2007).

3. Ibid.

4. Ibid.

5. Peter Gruss, National Museum of Emerging Science and Innovation Speech, The Max Planck Society for the Achievement of Science, Tokyo (September 15, 2005), Transcript, accessed March 26, 2007, http://www.mpg.de/pdf/redenPraesidenten/050915scienceTunnel_en.pdf.

6. John H. Holland, "What Is to Come and How to Predict It," in *The Next Fifty Years*, ed., John Brockman (New York: Vintage Books, 2002), 170–82.

7. Thomas L. Friedman, *The World Is Flat: A Brief History of the 21st Century* (New York: FSG, 2005).

8. Rod A. Beckstrom and Ori Brafman, *The Starfish and the Spider* (New York: Penguin Group, 2006).

9. Marshall McLuhan, *Understanding Media: The Extensions of Man* (New York: McGraw Hill, 1968).

Chapter 39

1. Energy Technology Perspectives; Scenarios and Strategies to 2050, published by IEA.

Chapter 53

1. Charles Singer, *A Short History of Biology* (1931).

Bibliography

Chapter 47

Ewald, Paul W., *Evolution of Infectious Disease*, Oxford Press, 1996.

Ewald, Paul W., *Plague Time: How Stealth Infections Cause Cancer, Heart Disease, and Other Deadly Ailments*, Free Press, 2000.

Greger, Michael, *Bird Flu: A Virus of Our Own Hatching*, Lantern Books, 2006.

Nikiforuk, Andrew, *Pandemonium: Bird Flu, Mad Cow Disease and Other Biological Plagues of the 21st Century*, Viking Canada, 2006.

Orent, Wendy, *Plague: The Mysterious Past and Terrifying Future of the World's Most Dangerous Disease*, Free Press, 2004.